THOMAS MERTON ON PEACE

MOWBRAYS

LONDON & OXFORD

*Printed in Great Britain by
Redwood Burn Limited
Trowbridge & Esher*

ISBN: 0 264 66339 X

*First published in Great Britain 1976
by A. R. Mowbray & Co. Limited,
The Alden Press, Osney Mead, Oxford OX2 0EG*

Contents

CONTENTS

I

PRINCIPLES
OF PEACE

Original Child Bomb

Points for meditation to be scratched on the walls of a cave

1: In the year 1945 an Original Child was born.
The name Original Child was given to it by
the Japanese people, who recognized that it was
the first of its kind.

2: On April 12th, 1945, Mr. Harry Truman
became the President of the United States,
which was then fighting the Second World War.
Mr. Truman was a vice president who became
President by accident when his predecessor died
of a cerebral hemorrhage. He did not know
as much about the war as the President before
him did. He knew a lot less about the war
than many people did.

About one hour after Mr. Truman became
President, his aides told him about a new bomb
which was being developed by atomic
scientists. They called it the "atomic bomb."
They said scientists had been working on it for
six years and that it had so far cost two
billion dollars. They added that its power was
equal to that of twenty thousand tons of
TNT. A single bomb could destroy a city. One of
those present added, in a reverent tone, that
the new explosive might eventually destroy the
whole world.

But Admiral Leahy told the President the
bomb would never work.

3: President Truman formed a committee of
men to tell him if this bomb would work, and if
so, what he should do with it. Some
members of this committee felt that the bomb
would jeopardize the future of civilization.
They were against its use. Others wanted it to
be used in demonstration on a forest of
cryptomeria trees, but not against a civil or
military target. Many atomic scientists warned
that the use of atomic power in war would
be difficult and even impossible to control. The
danger would be very great. Finally, there
were others who believed that if the bomb were
used just once or twice, on one or two Japanese
cities, there would be no more war. They
believed the new bomb would produce eternal
peace.

4: In June 1945 the Japanese government
was taking steps to negotiate for peace. On one
hand the Japanese ambassador tried to
interest the Russian government in acting as a
go-between with the United States. On the
other hand, an unofficial approach was made
secretly through Mr. Allen Dulles in Switzerland.
The Russians said they were not interested
and that they would not negotiate. Nothing was
done about the other proposal, which was
not official. The Japanese High Command was
not in favor of asking for peace, but wanted
to continue the war, even if the Japanese
mainland were invaded. The generals believed
that the war should continue until everybody
was dead. The Japanese generals were
professional soldiers.

5: In the same month of June, the President's
committee decided that the new bomb
should be dropped on a Japanese city. This
would be a demonstration of the bomb on a
civil and military target. As "demonstration" it
would be a kind of a "show." "Civilians"
all over the world love a good "show." The

"destructive" aspect of the bomb would
be "military."

6: The same committee also asked if America's
friendly ally, the Soviet Union, should be
informed of the atomic bomb. Someone
suggested that this information would make the
Soviet Union even more friendly than it was
already. But all finally agreed that the
Soviet Union was now friendly enough.

7: There was discussion about which city
should be selected as the first target. Some
wanted it to be Kyoto, an ancient capital
of Japan and a center of the Buddhist religion.
Others said no, this would cause bitterness.
As a result of a chance conversation, Mr.
Stimson, the Secretary of War, had recently
read up on the history and beauties of Kyoto. He
insisted that this city should be left untouched.
Some wanted Tokyo to be the first target,
but others argued that Tokyo had already been
practically destroyed by fire raids and
could no longer be considered a "target." So
it was decided Hiroshima was the most
opportune target, as it had not yet been bombed
at all. Lucky Hiroshima! What others had
experienced over a period of four years
would happen to Hiroshima in a single day!
Much time would be saved, and "time is
money!"

8: When they bombed Hiroshima they would
put the following out of business: the
Ube Nitrogen Fertilizer Company; the Ube Soda
Company; the Nippon Motor Oil Company;
the Sumitoma Chemical Company; the
Sumitoma Aluminum Company, and most of
the inhabitants.

9: At this time some atomic scientists
protested again, warning that the use of the
bomb in war would tend to make the
United States unpopular. But the President's
committee was by now fully convinced that the
bomb had to be used. Its use would arouse

the attention of the Japanese military class
and give them food for thought.

10: Admiral Leahy renewed his declaration that
the bomb would not explode.

11: On the 4th of July, when the United States
in displays of fireworks celebrates its
independence from British rule, the British and
Americans agreed together that the bomb
ought to be used against Japan.

12: On July 7th the Emperor of Japan
pleaded with the Soviet Government to act as
mediator for peace between Japan and the
Allies. Molotov said the question would
be "studied." In order to facilitate this "study"
Soviet troops in Siberia prepared to attack
the Japanese. The Allies had, in any case, been
urging Russia to join the war against Japan.
However, now that the atomic bomb was
nearly ready, some thought it would be better
if the Russians took a rest.

13: The time was coming for the new bomb to
be tested, in the New Mexico desert. A name
was chosen to designate this secret operation. It
was called "Trinity."

14: At 5:30 A.M. on July 16th, 1945, a
plutonium bomb was successfully exploded in
the desert at Alamogordo, New Mexico. It
was suspended from a hundred-foot steel tower
which evaporated. There was a fireball a
mile wide. The great flash could be seen for a
radius of 250 miles. A blind woman miles
away said she perceived light. There was a cloud
of smoke 40,000 feet high. It was shaped
like a toadstool.

15: Many who saw the experiment expressed
their satisfaction in religious terms. A
semi-official report even quoted a religious book
—the New Testament—"Lord, I believe, help
thou my unbelief." There was an atmosphere
of devotion. It was a great act of faith.

They believed the explosion was exceptionally
powerful.

16: Admiral Leahy, still a "doubting Thomas,"
said that the bomb would not explode when
dropped from a plane over a city. Others may
have had "faith," but he had his own variety of
"hope."

17: On July 21st a full written report of
the explosion reached President Truman at
Potsdam. The report was documented by
pictures. President Truman read the report and
looked at the pictures before starting out
for the conference. When he left his mood was
jaunty and his step was light.

18: That afternoon Mr. Stimson called on
Mr. Churchill, and laid before him a
sheet of paper bearing a code message about
the successful test. The message read
"Babies satisfactorily born." Mr. Churchill was
quick to realize that there was more in this
than met the eye. Mr. Stimson satisfied
his legitimate curiosity.

19: On this same day sixty atomic scientists who
knew of the test signed a petition that the
bomb should not be used against Japan
without a convincing warning and an
opportunity to surrender.

At this time the U.S.S. *Indianapolis*, which
had left San Francisco on the 18th, was
sailing toward the Island of Tinian, with some
U 235 in a lead bucket. The fissionable material
was about the size of a softball, but there
was enough for one atomic bomb. Instructions
were that if the ship sank, the uranium was
to be saved first, before any life. The
mechanism of the bomb was on board the U.S.S.
Indianapolis, but it was not yet assembled.

20: On July 26th the Potsdam declaration was
issued. An ultimatum was given to Japan:
"Surrender unconditionally or be destroyed."

Nothing was said about the new bomb. But
pamphlets dropped all over Japan
threatened "an enormous air bombardment"
if the army would not surrender. On July 26th
the U.S.S. *Indianapolis* arrived at Tinian and the
bomb was delivered.

21: On July 28th, since the Japanese High
Command wished to continue the war,
the ultimatum was rejected. A censored version
of the ultimatum appeared in the Japanese
press with the comment that it was "an
attempt to drive a wedge between the military
and the Japanese people." But the Emperor
continued to hope that the Russians, after
"studying" his proposal, would help to
negotiate a peace. On July 30th Mr. Stimson
revised a draft of the announcement that was to
be made after the bomb was dropped on the
Japanese target. The statement was much
better than the original draft.

22: On August 1st the bomb was assembled in an
airconditioned hut on Tinian. Those who
handled the bomb referred to it as "Little Boy."
Their care for the Original Child was devoted
and tender.

23: On August 2nd President Truman was
the guest of His Majesty King George VI
on board the H.M.S. *Renown* in Plymouth
Harbor. The atomic bomb was praised. Admiral
Leahy, who was present, declared that the
bomb would not work. His Majesty George VI
offered a small wager to the contrary.

24: On August 2nd a special message from the
Japanese Foreign Minister was sent to the
Japanese Ambassador in Moscow. "It is
requested that further efforts be exerted. . . .
Since the loss of one day may result in a
thousand years of regret, it is requested that you
immediately have a talk with Molotov."
But Molotov did not return from Potsdam until
the day the bomb fell.

25: On August 4th the bombing crew on Tinian
watched a movie of "Trinity" (the
Alamogordo Test). August 5th was a Sunday but
there was little time for formal worship.
They said a quick prayer that the war might end
"very soon." On that day, Col. Tibbetts,
who was in command of the B-29 that was to
drop the bomb, felt that his bomber ought
to have a name. He baptized it Enola Gay, after
his mother in Iowa. Col. Tibbetts was a well-
balanced man, and not sentimental. He did not
have a nervous breakdown after the bombing,
like some of the other members of the crew.

26: On Sunday afternoon "Little Boy"
was brought out in procession and devoutly
tucked away in the womb of Enola Gay.
That evening few were able to sleep. They were
as excited as little boys on Christmas Eve.

27: At 1:37 A.M. August 6th the weather scout
plane took off. It was named the Straight
Flush, in reference to the mechanical action of a
water closet. There was a picture of one,
to make this evident.

28: At the last minute before taking off, Col.
Tibbetts changed the secret radio call
sign from "Visitor" to "Dimples." The Bombing
Mission would be a kind of flying smile.

29: At 2:45 A.M. Enola Gay got off the ground
with difficulty. Over Iwo Jima she met her
escort, two more B-29s, one of which was called
the Great Artiste. Together they proceeded
to Japan.

30: At 6:40 they climbed to 31,000 feet, the
bombing altitude. The sky was clear. It was a
perfect morning.

31: At 3:09 they reached Hiroshima and
started the bomb run. The city was full of sun.
The fliers could see the green grass in
the gardens. No fighters rose up to meet them.

There was no flak. No one in the city
bothered to take cover.

32: The bomb exploded within 100 feet of the
aiming point. The fireball was 18,000 feet
across. The temperature at the center of
the fireball was 100,000,000 degrees. The
people who were near the center became
nothing. The whole city was blown to bits and
the ruins all caught fire instantly
everywhere, burning briskly. 70,000 people
were killed right away or died within a
few hours. Those who did not die at once
suffered great pain. Few of them were soldiers.

33: The men in the plane perceived that the
raid had been successful, but they thought of
the people in the city and they were not
perfectly happy. Some felt they had
done wrong. But in any case they had obeyed
orders. "It was war."

34: Over the radio went the code message that
the bomb had been successful: "Visible
effects greater than Trinity. . . . Proceeding to
Papacy." Papacy was the code name for Tinian.

35: It took a little while for the rest of Japan
to find out what had happened to Hiroshima.
Papers were forbidden to publish any
news of the new bomb. A four-line item said
that Hiroshima had been hit by incendiary
bombs and added: "It seems that some damage
was caused to the city and its vicinity."

36: Then the military governor of the
Prefecture of Hiroshima issued a proclamation
full of martial spirit. To all the people
without hands, without feet, with their faces
falling off, with their intestines hanging
out, with their whole bodies full of radiation,
he declared: "We must not rest a single day in
our war effort. . . . We must bear in mind
that the annihilation of the stubborn enemy is
our road to revenge." He was a
professional soldier.

37: On August 8th Molotov finally summoned the
Japanese Ambassador. At last neutral
Russia would give an answer to the Emperor's
inquiry. Molotov said coldly that the Soviet
Union was declaring war on Japan.

38: On August 9th another bomb was dropped
on Nagasaki, though Hiroshima was still
burning. On August 11th the Emperor
overruled his high command and accepted the
peace terms dictated at Potsdam. Yet for three
days discussion continued, until on August
14th the surrender was made public and final.

39: Even then the Soviet troops thought
they ought to fight in Manchuria "just a little
longer." They felt that even though they could
not, at this time, be of help in Japan, it
would be worthwhile if they displayed their
goodwill in Manchuria, or even in Korea.

40: As to the Original Child that was now born,
President Truman summed up the philosophy
of the situation in a few words. "We found
the bomb," he said, "and we used it."

41: Since that summer many other bombs have
been "found." What is going to happen?
At the time of writing, after a season of brisk
speculation, men seem to be fatigued by the
whole question.

Peace and Protest:

A Statement

If a pacifist is one who believes that all war is always morally wrong and always has been wrong, then I am not a pacifist. Nevertheless I see war as an avoidable tragedy and I believe that the problem of solving international conflict without massive violence has become the number one problem of our time. As President Kennedy said, "If we do not end war, war is going to end us." Pope John XXIII, Pope Paul VI, have said this with all the solemn authority of their position. The task of man and of the Church is to end all wars, to provide a satisfactory international power to police the world and subdue violence while conflicts are settled by reason and negotiation. Therefore the entire human race has a most serious obligation to face this problem and to do something about it. Each one of us has to resist an ingrained tendency to violence and to destructive thinking. But every time we renounce reason and patience in order to solve a conflict by violence we are side-stepping this great obligation and putting it off. How long can we continue to do this? Our time is limited, and we are not taking advantage of our opportunities.

The human race today is like an alcoholic who knows that drink will destroy him and yet always has "good reasons" why he must continue drinking. Such is man in his fatal addiction to war. He is not really capable of seeing a constructive alternative to war.

If this task of building a peaceful world is the most important task of our time, it is also the most difficult. It will, in fact, require far more discipline, more sacrifice, more planning, more thought, more cooperation and more heroism than war ever demanded.

The task of ending war is in fact the greatest challenge to human courage and intelligence. Can we meet this challenge? Do we have the moral strength and the faith that are required? Sometimes the prospect seems almost hopeless, for man is more addicted to violence now than he ever has been before, and we are today spending more for war alone than we spent for everything, war included, thirty years ago. We also live in a crisis of faith in which to most men "God is dead" and even some Christians no longer accept Christ except as a symbol.

I do not advocate the burning of draft cards. It is not my opinion that the draft law is so unjust that it calls for civil disobedience. But nevertheless I believe that we must admit patriotic dissent and argument at a time like this. Such dissent must be responsible. It must give a clear and reasonable account of itself to the nation, and it must help sincere and concerned minds to accept alternatives to war without surrendering the genuine interests of our own national community. This dissent should not be ambiguous or threatening.

There is considerable danger of ambiguity in protests that seek mainly to capture the attention of the press and to gain publicity for a cause, being more concerned with their impact upon the public than with the meaning of that impact. Such dissent tends to be at once dramatic and superficial. It may cause a slight commotion, but in a week everything is forgotten—some new shock has occurred in some other area. What is needed is a constructive dissent that recalls people to their senses, makes them think deeply, plants in them a seed of change, and awakens in them the profound need for truth, reason and peace which is implanted in·man's nature. Such dissent implies belief in openness of mind and in the possibility of mature exchange of ideas. When protest becomes desperate and seemingly extreme, then perhaps one reason for this is that the ones protesting have given up hope of a fair hearing, and therefore seek only to shock or to horrify. On the other hand, perhaps the public is too eager to be shocked and horrified, and to refuse a fair hearing. The reaction of shock seems to dispense us from serious thought. This is a problem for all of us now. We are Americans, and we have a duty to live up to our heritage of open-mindedness. We must always be tolerant and fair and never persecute others for their opinions. The way to silence error is by truth, not by violence. But we will always prefer violence to truth if our imaginations are at every moment overstimulated by frenzied and dangerous fantasies.

Therefore one of the most important tasks of the moment is to recognize the great problem of the *mental climate* in which we live. Our minds are filled with images which call for violent and erratic reactions. We can hardly recover our senses long enough to think calmly and make reasoned commitments. We are swept by alternate fears and hopes which have no relation to deep moral truth. A protest which merely compounds these fears and hopes with a new store of images can hardly help us become men of peace.

The great value of Pope Paul's visit to the United Nations was precisely this: it was a positive and constructive witness which, together with a clear and firm protest against war and injustice, reawakened a definite hope in peaceful alternatives to war. It was a most serious and highly credible reminder that instruments for peaceful conflict solution are at hand. These instruments are abused and discredited, but if men *want to* make serious and effective use of them, they are still free to do so.

All protest against war and all witness for peace should in some way or other strive to overcome the desperation and hopelessness with which man now, in fact, regards all his existing peace-making machinery as futile and beyond redemption. It is this practical despair of effective peace-making that drives man more and more to embrace the conclusion that only war is effective and that because violence seems to pay off, we must finally resort to it.

Is it perhaps this insatiable hunger for visible and quick returns that has driven the majority of Americans to accept the war in Vietnam as reasonable? Are we so psychologically constituted and determined that we find real comfort in a daily score of bombed bridges and burned villages, forgetting that the price of our psychological security is the burned flesh of women and children who have no guilt and no escape from the fury of our weapons?

One thing that gives such a drastic character to the protest against war is the realization which the peace people have of this unjust suffering inflicted on the innocent largely as a result of our curious inner psychological needs, fomented by the climate of our culture.

In order to resist this appeal to mercy, those who want and "need" the violence in Vietnam disregard the sufferings of "the enemy" and concentrate on the very real and desperate hardships of our own GIs in Vietnam.

Yet there remains a difference:

The sufferings of our own men are avoidable. There are alternatives. It is even possible that these alternatives would be more effective and would restore the honor of our country in the eyes of those nations that feel threatened by us and therefore hate us.

Can we not keep open in our minds the possibility of seeking these alternatives? Can our government not divert some of the money paid out for our overkill capacity, to investigate the chances of lasting and realistic peace? Or will we continue to abandon ourselves to the flow of immediate reactions and superficial events, with no plan and no hope for an intelligible future, content only to wring some practical and visible effect by the use of violence from a confused and unintelligible present?

Let there be no mistake about the end to which this road leads. It is man's ruin, degradation and dishonor.

Christianity and Defense in the Nuclear Age

We have to recognize that the chief deficiency in theological evaluations of our present situation is that we have not at all caught up with the realities of our time. Our task at present cannot possibly be one of arriving at *clear and definite* solutions. It must first of all be a matter of estimating the work to be done, clearing ground, readjusting our views to the essentially new, tragically critical situation in which the entire human race finds itself. As Christians first of all, in a crisis where the very existence of man and the continuation of life itself are at stake, our duty to God the Creator becomes a duty to strive in every way to preserve and protect His creation. Our duty is to help save humanity for which Christ died. We cannot contemn man, or disregard his plight, and allege loyalty to abstract beliefs as an excuse, still less as a *reason* for policies based on hatred and destructiveness. To "kill Commies for Christ" is to admit that one has lost all sense of the meaning of the gospel of Christ.

It is in view of this task that we must first of all clearly state, not as a solution to problems, but as a prerequisite for considering the problem in its reality: that it is the unanimous judgment of *all* really serious religious, philosophical, social, psychological thought today that *total war* (whether nuclear or conventional) is both immoral and suicidal. This is so clear that it seems to require little discussion or proof. For a Catholic, there are the very clear statements of Pius XII and John XXIII. Even the theologians, whether Catholic or Protestant, who still insist that *war itself* can still be resorted to as a solution to international conflicts, and who therefore recommend strong military measures of defense, agree in practice that *total war* must be condemned not only as immoral but also as impractical and self-defeating. All who have a serious knowledge of the power of nuclear weapons and the extreme danger of the situation that has been created by the Cold War and the arms race realize that resort to a nuclear attack would unleash destruction which probably neither antagonist would survive.

This does not prevent politicians, and entire nations, from supporting a colossal war effort, on a scale never before dreamed of. It does not prevent the masses of "Christian" people from *taking it for granted* that nuclear war is not only a reasonable but even a Christian solution to the problem of Communism, at least in the sense that while no one "wants war," there is an inescapable necessity to act in a warlike and "tough" manner, to preserve our way of life and indeed our religion itself. It must be noticed that in doing this, Christians are actually aligning themselves with pragmatists for whom the moral issue is totally irrelevant. In taking this line of thought, Christians are working with the forces which are, in fact, most inimical to Christianity.

The problem, on the practical level, is urgent.

It is one in which Christians are and must be deeply involved. It is the problem of evaluating *the critical situation of humanity* in its totality, so that we may see the one problem of war in its whole context, and may also be able to work toward alternative solutions to international and national problems. It is a matter of primary urgency to see our way clear to other solutions than those presently being worked out by the military, by industry, and by the politicians who follow the suggestions and exhortations of the military-industrial complex.

The Christian has a duty, as a Christian, to contribute everything he can to help this great common work: *of finding nonmilitary and nonviolent ways of defending our rights, our interests, and our ideals.*

And yet in actual fact it seems that Christians, as much as anybody else, are contributing very much to the dangerous tensions and the irrational state of mind which is obsessed with the fear of disaster and is fixated on one hope: nuclear defense. It is Christians who are, as loudly as anyone else, clamoring for an unbeatable missile defense system—all of course in the name of "peace." And it is Christians who, as much as anybody else, are refusing even to consider possible alternatives to this line of action. It is Christians who most loudly and passionately support policies of overkill.

The following very schematic notes are an outline of a few approaches to the problem. They are more an evaluation of present modes of thought than a constructive program of change. We have to begin at the bottom, we are very poor in ideas and insights, we have barely started to wake up to our position.

One thing is very certain: inadequate and worn-out ideas must be discarded. Importance of our thinking and our information. Importance of a public opinion that is not fanatical and wild, but informed by reasonable as well as Christian principles and looking toward a worldwide cooperation in solving the critical problems of our time. We must recognize that fanatical nationalism and racism are prime causes of moral blindness—especially when they appeal most stridently to "moral principles."

1. *Imperfect Approaches:*

We rule out at the start all the extreme, fanatical, bellicose solutions. On the side of those who work for peace:

a. The conventional "pacifist" position is inadequate, if by this we mean a peace movement of individuals associated in a protest based on personal objections of conscience.

   Not a question of individual conscience alone.

   A problem for all men, a worldwide social question. Protest is not enough. Objection not enough. Personal withdrawal not enough.

b. A radical and sweeping policy of "unilateral disarmament." It is naïve, and would do more harm than good. Takes no account of important realities: the state of shock in which millions of people already are, and which would be magnified thousands of times over if the "only means of defense" were suddenly taken away. Might precipitate a war. On the other hand *unilateral initiatives* in *gradual* steps toward disarmament are imperative. These steps must be serious and courageous, and we must realize that they would add greatly to the prestige of the nation that could make them a sign of confidence, determination and strength. But such strength implies *alternatives* to military defense.

c. A purely "spiritual" witness. Is not enough. Simply to stand up and say that the world is wicked and is traveling toward an apocalyptic doom, and that the Christian is an individual witness, or the Church is a witness purely and simply calling man to repentance before it is too late. This is not enough. We must certainly bring the world to repentance, but we must engage with the rest of mankind in a collaborative work of social renewal, reconciliation, in a serious effort to bring about a peaceful world situation, in which men can work together to solve the enormous social problems posed by the technological and economic revolution of our time.

d. The "Just War"—"We must maintain peace, but we must also maintain justice." Characteristic of American theological thought, both Protestant and Catholic, is the idea that the *presence of nuclear weapons does nothing to alter the traditional just war theory.* I am not a "pacifist" in the sense that I would reject even the *theory* of the just war. I agree that even today a just war might *theoretically* be possible. But I also think we must take into account a totally new situation in which the danger of any war escalating to all-out proportions makes it imperative to find other ways of resolving international conflicts. In practice the just war theory has become irrelevant.

   Niebuhr and Dunn: Let us examine their position. They

claim a "just war" is still possible and demand a strong defensive posture (military). Yet they make the following admissions:

    i. The only form of just war they envisage is a *limited* war *of defense aimed at "preventing conquest and forcing an end of hostilities."* No war aiming to bring about the "unconditional surrender and punishment of aggression" can fit (they declare) this definition of a "just war." Presumably the action of Kennedy in the Cuba crisis fits the definition.

[*A Personal Opinion on the Cuba Crisis:* Conflict cannot be avoided. And at the present time the threat of violence in conflict is also to be expected. The fact that this is a "necessary" evil does not excuse us from trying our best to get into a situation where violence will NOT be so necessary and so imminent. Actually Kennedy's action was extremely risky. It nearly precipitated a nuclear war, and could have done so. But at the same time it can be said that it perhaps forestalled a nuclear war (the American military might have become exceedingly trigger-happy if a lot of missile bases were operative in Cuba). It is useless to expect all problems to be suddenly solved innocently without further ado. But are we going in the right direction at all? This was perhaps a "solution" of sorts, but it must not be regarded as *adequate* and taken as a pattern or precedent.]

    ii. Niebuhr and Dunn then *exclude* a nuclear crusade against Communism and indeed the current war thinking does not clearly seem to fit their formula. Yet in effect they *are giving support* to the policies of Washington as they now are, in all their ambiguity. Hence their qualifications about limited war are practically irrelevant.

2. *A quick look at the military policies, and some of the contradictions involved for a Christian:*

    a. *Counterforce*—Theoretically this is a nuclear policy which can more easily be made to fit the moral theology books. It is a policy of preemptive attack on the enemy's missile bases (not on his cities). ACTUALLY IT IS THE MOST DANGEROUS POLICY. It is the one more and more favored in Washington, and the one which promises the most serious risk of preemptive first strike on the part of the enemy. And the inevitable consequences.

    b. *Deterrence*—The idea of threatening enemy cities from invulnerable missile sites. This might be harder to reconcile with the moral theology books, because the targets are frankly cities. But then the idea is that the missiles will "never be used." In practice, the missile sites invite preemptive first strike.

    c. In actual fact, both policies are in full swing (the "Mix").

        To support these policies is in effect to become a partner in extremely dangerous actions which, in the opinion of scientists like Leo Szilard, will lead to war within the next ten years. *Nuclear* war!

Note also the possibility of nuclear accidents, miscalculation, unintended acts of war.

Note some other ambiguities in our policy situation:

Our commitment to defend Berlin, which cannot possibly be defended with conventional weapons. Ergo: practical commitment to use of nuclear weapons even to "save face" if "necessary."

Note also: the theoretician who splits hairs about "just war" and makes nice distinctions in journals for experts is actually supporting the military mind and military policies, which imply no such fine distinctions at all.

We know that the military mind has one objective: to WIN at all costs. To completely subdue the adversary. This is common to extremists on both sides.

This is the thinking of the people who have the weapons on both sides.

The theologians may have nice thoughts about just war.

The military are above all concerned with *not being soft*, not showing fear, not being intimidated, not losing face.

This game of chicken by politicians and strategists is abetted and supported by Christians as a whole.

The state of affairs is this: men with nuclear weapons will use them when they think the situation is sufficiently critical. And they will not use them with any regard for restraints demanded by moral theologians.

To cooperate with them *now* is to share in their responsibility *then*.

3. *Summary of the Policy Situation:*

In theory our government rejects recourse to total nuclear war. We do not have a "policy of total war," the all-out destruction of Russia or China (though some extremists favor even that).

But the "mix" and the arms race add up, in fact, to a policy of total war. A policy of total war and unconditional victory is immoral and suicidal. What is essentially a power struggle is presented as an ideological and spiritual struggle, as a battle between light and darkness, and it is presented in such a way that CHRISTIANS ARE CONVINCED THERE IS NO OTHER WAY OF DEFENSE THAN MILITARY DEFENSE, that the surest defense is a fantastic arms build-up, and that the "strategists know best."

Hence it is taken for granted that any questioning of the present policies for defense is an implicit treason both to democracy and to Christianity. In actual fact, the first job we have is to open the way to clear thinking and investigation of *other methods of defense*.

It is definitely not a matter of renouncing defense, of giving in to Communism. It must be made quite clear that we intend to defend our ideals and our freedom. But that we also as Christians reject a form of defense which has now clearly become immoral and suicidal (we should have known this about war long ago, the First World War told us all we needed to know if earlier wars had not). And as Christians we want to take the lead in helping to discover the efficacy of *nonviolent methods of defense*.

4. *The Study of Alternatives:*
   a. Realize what we are up against. The military-industrial-political-academic complex, with the mass media at its disposal, is sold on military defense and the arms race and is obviously interested in ridiculing or discrediting all nonmilitary forms of defense—in fact all alternatives to the arms race.

      International negotiation for peace cannot be taken fully seriously in this climate, where it is assumed there is *no* alternative to nuclear armament on a colossal scale.
   b. Realize, however, that in the presence of formidable opposition and mistrust we must mobilize for the preservation of the human race, by a transformation of all the attitudes and methods that now govern our thought and action in politics.

      Christian thinking has to transform political attitudes!

      This means overcoming the "split" between the sacred and the profane, the spiritual and the political.
   c. We have got to get people to face the *moral evil* of nuclear war, and see the full moral and spiritual dimensions of the problem.
   d. We have got to support every kind of action that involves:
      —serious dialogue
      —genuine reciprocity
      —international understanding
      —social justice: removal of *causes* of war and unrest.
   e. We have got to see the spiritual and psychological evils in our own current social situation as a vitally important part of the problem:
      —boredom
      —tension
      —affluence
      —individualism and irresponsibility
   f. Study the positive meaning of nonviolent defense:
      —its *efficacy* as defense
      —its *clarity* in stating our will to resist
      —its *opportunities* for heroism and dedication.

Target Equals City[1]

There is one winner, only one winner, in war. The winner is war itself.
Not truth, not justice, not liberty, not morality. These are the van-
quished. War wins, reducing them to complete submission. He makes
truth serve violence and falsehood. He causes justice to declare not
what is just but what is expedient as well as cruel. He reduces the
liberty of the victorious side to a servitude equal to that of the tyranny
which they attacked, in defense of liberty. Though moralists may intend and endeavor to lay down rules for war, in the end war lays
down rules for them. He does not find it hard to make them change
their minds. If he could, he would change God's own mind. War has
power to transmute evil into good and good into evil. Do not fear
that he will not exercise this power. Now more than ever he is omni-
potent. He is the great force, the evil mystery, the demonic mover of
our century, with his globe of sun-fire, and his pillar of cloud. Worship him.

It took five years for war to turn the Christian ethic of the "just war"
inside out. The years 1940 to 1945 completely revolutionized the moral
thinking of the allies who were fighting totalitarianism with a *just
cause* if ever there was one.

Certainly no cause can be absolutely just and pure. You can always
find something wrong with it. But for those who accepted the traditional doctrine on war, there was not much doubt that Hitler was the
aggressor, and that we were the defenders.

When the Japanese bombed Pearl Harbor, there was no question
about the morality of America's entering the war to defend its rights.

1. The facts in this article are taken mostly from a recent detailed study of
the events which shaped the decision to use the A-bomb at the end of World
War II. *The Irreversible Decision, 1939–1950* by Robert C. Batchelder
(Houghton Mifflin) is a clear and persuasive plea for a clear and definite
ethical stand in regard to nuclear war, in place of the vague and unprincipled
pragmatism which guides decisions today. Our meditation can serve as a
review and a recommendation of this book.

Here was a very clear example of a "just cause" for war. Few doubted the fact. Those who did so were regarded as foolish because they were against all war on principle. They thought war was intrinsically evil. Twenty years later one is tempted to wonder if they were not more wise than men believed them to be.

At the end of World War II, many theologians openly began to discuss the question whether the old doctrine of the just war had any meaning. It seemed to them at that time that the obliteration bombing of cities on both sides, culminating in the total destruction of Hiroshima and Nagasaki by one plane with one bomb for each, had completely changed the nature of war. Traditional standards no longer applied because, for one thing, there was no longer any distinction made between civilian and combatant. Where this distinction was obliterated, or tended to be obliterated, war could not be considered just. Double effect could no longer be taken seriously when you "permitted" (without intending it) the slaughter of fifty thousand civilians in order to stop production in three or four factories. There was no proportion between the "permitted" evil and the "intended" good. (Investigation showed that even when there had been massive damage and countless deaths inflicted by obliteration bombing, the factories themselves were not always crippled for very long, and soon resumed production.)

Double effect was completely out of the question when the slaughter of civilians was explicitly *intended* as a means to "breaking enemy morale" and thus breaking his "will to resist." This was pure terrorism, and the traditional doctrine of war excluded such immoral methods. Traditional morality also excluded torture of prisoners, murder of hostages chosen at random, extermination of racial groups for no reason other than race, etc. These methods were practiced by the enemy, and after the war ended *they were bequeathed to the Western nations.* France in Algeria, for instance.

How did precision bombing, (allowed by traditional standards of justice) turn into obliteration bombing? How did ethical theory gradually come to defend obliteration bombing, and even mass destruction by atomic weapons? How did we gradually reach our present position where the traditional doctrine of the just war has been so profoundly modified that it is almost unrecognizable? How is it that we are now almost ready to permit any outrage, any excess, any horror, on the grounds that it is a "lesser evil" and "necessary" to save our nation?

The deliberate terroristic annihilation of defenseless civilians for military and political purposes, is perhaps not completely new. In all ages there has been calculated terrorism, the slaughter of innocents in war. It was never seriously considered as either very necessary or very useful in the actual process of winning a war. It was more or less of a "bonus." (You remember perhaps the report on the raid that annihilated Dresden? The city was full of refugees fleeing from the Russians in the east. The death of several thousand extra victims was announced with sober joy as a "bonus" by those who commanded the raid.)

Traditional Christian teaching, which deplored war itself even under the best of conditions, never hesitated to condemn terrorism in war as a very grave crime. Now terrorism is no longer taken so seriously. It has become "necessary," the "only effective defense," and of course defense is a "duty." Hence we are seriously told that it is the "duty" of our government to arm to the teeth with nuclear weapons capable of wiping out whole cities, whole nations. A conservative estimate declares that the United States probably now stocks the equivalent in explosive power of *ten tons of TNT for every human being on the face of the earth*. We are generously going beyond the limits of strict duty, just in case.

Terror from the air, as a deliberately planned policy, was characteristic of the Nazi and Fascist Axis. As a matter of fact the honor of having initiated it in Europe belongs to Catholic nations: Franco's Spain and Fascist Italy. The place? Guernica, a Christian city, in the Christian province of the Basques, in Christian Spain. Date: 1937. Also please remember Nanking, China. Same year. Not so many Christians. We protested.

Poland was the next victim. Reduced to nothing in a few days by the Luftwaffe. 1939. England came next.

It is to the everlasting credit of the British that although the civilians of England suffered one crushing blow after another, and saw whole sections of their cities reduced to rubble, the government declared that the RAF would abide by traditional methods, and would confine itself to the strategic bombing of military targets only. But since daylight raids were very costly, most of the attacks had to be carried out at night. This made precision bombing very difficult, and in the end civilians suffered more than industry. So "area bombing," the destruction of the whole neighborhood that included a military target, was already British policy by the time America came into the war. America determined to stick to the traditional ethical code. Roosevelt at first announced that the AAF would confine itself to strategic bombing.

By 1942, however, England abandoned its quixotic attachment to standards which were simply preventing the RAF raids from being fully effective. At least that was what the RAF thought. It was Air Marshal Sir Arthur Travers Harris who opened up with obliteration bombing against German cities in 1942. Not only was this aimed at the "sure" destruction of factories and military objectives that might otherwise be missed, but frankly and explicitly the intention was to "destroy enemy morale." "There are no lengths in violence to which we will not go" to achieve this end, declared Churchill. And another government spokesman, unidentified, said, "Our plans are to bomb, burn and ruthlessly destroy, in every way available to us, the people responsible for creating this war."

Here we have already one complete cycle. A country begins a defensive "just war." It starts by declaring its firm adherence to the ethical principles held by its Church, and by the majority of its civilian population. The nation accepts unjust suffering heroically. But then the military begins to grow impatient, seeing that its own methods of retaliation are not effective. It is *the military that changes the policy.* The new, more ruthless policy pays off. The civilian protest is silenced before it begins. Those who might otherwise have objected come to believe what they are told: "This will save lives. It is necessary to end the war sooner, and to punish the unjust aggressor."

The standards of justice are still in view—still *partially* in view. The injustice of the aggressor is very clearly seen. Justice in the use of means has been lost sight of, and what counts most is expediency.

We cannot lightly blame the courageous people who suffered so much and were so eager for the war to end. But . . . The allies had come around to adopting the same methods precisely, the same ruthless inhumanity which made the enemy unjust. Injustice was now common to both sides. Needless to say, both were now strenuously arguing and convincing themselves, in exactly the same terms, that their war effort was just, that their methods were just, and that it was necessary to do all that they did in order to win the victory, end the war quickly and "save lives."

Note also, on both sides there were sincere Catholics, encouraged by the clergy and by the Catholic press to accept and support these claims. There were therefore Catholics believing that each side was completely just. Catholics on both sides "served God" by killing each other. . . . What had become of the meaning of the doctrine of the "just war"? What had become of Christian ethics in this situation? Did anyone stop to reflect on the total absurdity of this self-contradiction on the part of Christians? Not the least appalling contradiction lay in the fact that German Christians heroically sacrificed themselves to defend a government that cruelly persecuted the Church. In defense of Hitler's neopaganism which advocated a totally immoral policy they fought their fellow Christians of France, England and America.

Just war? Just cause? Just methods? Double effect?

Now America was in the war. America was obviously going to follow the tactics England had been forced to take over from the Nazis by the very logic of the war. The USAF soon began obliteration bombing. A protest was published in *Fellowship,* the magazine of the Fellowship of Reconciliation, in 1944. Obliteration bombing was condemned by this magazine and by a group of Protestant ministers. The protest was taken seriously enough to get an official reply. Roosevelt said that these tactics were necessary to "shorten the war." There was a nationwide discussion of the issue. Americans were fifty to one against those who protested. They thought the moral scruples of these pacifists were ridiculous. To demand cessation of obliteration bombing was pure defeatism.

All distinction between precision bombing and obliteration bombing was forgotten in the general indignation. What mattered was to beat Hitler and right the wrong that had been done. Any methods that helped procure this end were justifiable.

One dissenting voice was that of a Catholic priest, Father John C. Ford, S.J., who argued that the obliteration bombing of cities was immoral and could not be defended by the principle of double effect.

Meanwhile the United States was working feverishly to develop the atomic bomb, believing that Hitler's scientists were on the point of perfecting this weapon that would multiply thousands of times the destructiveness of ordinary bombing.

However, before the atomic bomb was tested, the B29 bomber command in the Pacific had come to realize the failure of precision bombing of Japanese military targets. It was not possible to seriously slow down production by this means.

Early in 1945, General Curtis LeMay decided, on his own responsibility, to initiate a devastating new tactic of massive low-flying fire raids delivered at night.

On the night of March 9–10 the whole of Tokyo was set afire with napalm bombs. The blaze was so furious that it boiled the water of the canals. Fire storms consumed all the oxygen, and many who were not burned to death suffocated. So frightful were the effects of this raid that it claimed as many casualties as the Atom bombing of Hiroshima.

Some apologists for all-out war point to this fact, saying that since there is in reality no difference between total war carried on by conventional weapons and total war carried on by nuclear weapons, there is no new moral issue involved. On the contrary, this calls for a clarification of the real moral issue. The issue is precisely this: not that atomic and nuclear weapons are immoral while conventional weapons are just, but that *any resort to terrorism and total annihilation is unjust, whatever be the weapons it employs.*

The Tokyo raid, followed by similar raids on more than fifty other Japanese cities, was justified on the grounds that much of the Japanese war effort depended on the "phantom industry," the detailed piecework on small parts carried on by individuals in their homes. Hence residential areas came to be just as "legitimate" a target as factories themselves. This fact contributed to the loose generalization, now widely accepted, without further qualifications, that "in modern war everyone is to be considered a combatant." Hence even residential areas became "military targets." No more need for double effect!

Already in May and June of 1945 the American High Command was considering the choice of an appropriate target for the new bomb.

In discussing the choice of target, Truman and his advisers did not speak of this or that naval base, this or that fortress, this or that concentration of troops, this or that particular munitions plant. In Truman's own words: "Stimson's staff had *prepared a list of cities* in

Japan that might serve as targets. . . ." Later in the context Truman speaks of the entire city of Hiroshima as a "military target."

We must remember that in the list of cities originally considered was Kyoto, which is a religious and not a military center at all.

There were, of course, industries at Hiroshima, but its "military" importance was such that it had hardly been touched so far. It had even been neglected by LeMay's incendiaries.

In other words, the "targets" considered for the Atomic bomb were purely and simply cities. Any city at all, by the mere fact of being a city, was now a "military target." The fact that Kyoto was among them indicates that moral and psychological effect, in other words terrorism, was the dominant consideration in the minds of the high command.

Hiroshima was chosen in order that an "untouched" target might show the power of the bomb. The idea was to unleash the maximum destructive power on a civilian center, to obliterate that center and destroy all further will to resist in the Japanese nation. The word "target" and the word "city" had become completely identified.

Once again, moral thinking had gone through a full cycle in the short space of two or three years. The United States had entered the war with the conviction of the justice of its cause and with the firm intention to abide by just means.

However, it is possible that the notion of "just means" was much more nebulous in the American mind than it had been in the English. Moral thinking guided by pragmatic principles tends to be very vague, very fluid. Moral decisions were now a series of more or less opportunistic choices based on short-term guesses of possible consequences, rather than on definite moral principles.

It is quite certain that though the American public conscience was characterized by a certain undefined sense of decency and fittingness in these matters, a sense more or less attributable to the vestiges of Christian tradition, this "moral sense" easily yielded to the more practical dictates of the situation.

The moral decision to use the bomb, without warning, on a Japanese city was dictated by the urgent desire to end the war promptly, without having to sacrifice thousands of American combatants in the planned invasion of the Japanese archipelago. Once again, the idea was "to punish the unjust aggressor" and to "save American lives." Certainly few Americans, before the bomb was dropped, would have questioned the validity of these considerations. The war had to be ended, and this was the way to do it.

It was not generally known that Japan was trying to establish diplomatic contacts with the allies through Russia in order to work out a negotiated peace instead of the unconditional surrender relentlessly demanded by the allies. Neither invasion of Japan nor use of the bomb was absolutely necessary for peace. However, the war mentality of the time made it impossible for policy-makers to see this. They were con--

vinced the bomb was necessary and their conviction overwhelmed all other considerations.

Nevertheless the use of the bomb on two open cities was a dire injustice and an atrocity.

Even after the war ended, a questionnaire conducted by *Fortune* revealed that half the respondents felt the decision to use the bomb on Hiroshima and Nagasaki had been right, while nearly a quarter of them *regretted that more atomic bombs* had not been used on other Japanese cities! Such was, and is, the general moral climate in the U.S.A.

At the same time, the terrible effects of the bomb produced a moral shock and profound revulsions in certain quarters in America. Religious groups and publications protested more or less vehemently. Catholic voices, notably those of the *Commonweal*, the *Catholic World* and, of course, the *Catholic Worker* were raised against the "sin" of the bomb. But it is to be noted that *America* already took a much more "realistic" and complacent view of the event.

In general, articulate protest against the bomb on moral grounds has been confined to a minority. The majority of Americans have "sincerely regretted" the necessity to use it, they have, in a word, "felt bad" about it. But that is all. These decent sentiments have very easily yielded to other, more "practical" considerations, and the foreign policy of our country since Hiroshima, while occasionally making perfunctory gestures of respect in the direction of the Deity, has been a policy of direct reliance on the threat of atomic and nuclear annihilation.

There have of course been repeated statements of unwillingness to carry out these threats, on the vague grounds that the consequences would be too awful. The American mind in general has, however, not questioned the fundamental propriety of using the bomb. This is practically taken for granted.

As the pressures of the cold war become more intense, the fallout shelter scare has had a direct and intimate connection with the policy of nuclear deterrence. It has been clearly and explicitly part of a campaign to "engineer consent" and make nuclear war thoroughly acceptable, at least as a reasonable possibility, in the American public mind. This, in turn, is intended to convince our enemies that we "believe in" the bomb, and that, though we still utter pious hopes that it will never be necessary, we thoroughly intend to use it if we feel ourselves to be sufficiently threatened.

Here, then, is the moral situation:

1. There has been a complete breakdown in the old notion of the "just war" as accepted for centuries by Christian ethics and international law. As far as policy-makers are concerned, this concept has now become completely irrelevant. It has been supplanted by the concept of "limited war," which has no ethical connotations, but is simply "tactical" and is designed to avoid the more disastrous effects of an

all-out war of annihilation. The "value" of a limited war, with or without tactical nuclear weapons, is that there is more of a chance that it may theoretically be "won" by one side or the other. At the same time, there seems to be every reason to believe that if one of the belligerents feels himself to be losing a limited war, he will resort to retaliation on the megatonic scale, and the war will become "total."

2. Moralists, while still clinging more or less resolutely to the idea that obliteration of civilian centers is evil (some show very little resolution in their attachment to this principle!) strive in general to patch up the traditional notion of just war and keep it functioning, by tying it up with the "limited" war of the tacticians. This ends by being a rather Pickwickian position, and in actual fact the moralists who still try to reconcile traditional notions with the new situation seek means of justifying massive nuclear retaliation as "self-defense."

Though no clear official pronouncement in this matter has been made by the Church, the repeated warnings of the Popes and their strong pleas for peace have insisted on the traditional principle that the rights of unarmed and noncombatant civilians must be respected and that failure to take these rights into account is a grave crime. Military policy, on the other hand, has completely discarded all consideration of these rights, except in perfunctory statements designed to assuage the scruples of the old-fashioned.

Theologians remain divided, but a strong and articulate group, especially in Europe, have taken their stand on the "relative pacifist" position which would outlaw all nuclear war and work for disarmament as the course of action most consistent with Christian morality.

It must be confessed that these issues are not as widely or as thoroughly discussed as they might be. The relative pacifist position does not get a very good hearing in the press, especially in the United States. The average Catholic is left with the impression that nuclear deterrence and the annihilation of Russian cities by H-bombs is *encouraged* by the Church, or at least left indifferently to the judgment of governments and military commands. The Church is by no means indifferent on this point. This fact is obscured because the moral thinking not only of the Christian laity but also of the clergy has been seriously confused by the mass media.

The Christian moral sense is being repeatedly eroded and worn down by the effect of the "cycles" we have described. A new policy is adopted on grounds that appear to be fully "just." Then, when the "ethical" means are found to be less expedient, more drastic measures are resorted to. Those violate justice, but the justification of them by publicists further weakens the moral sense of Christians. Occasional shocks momentarily reawaken this moral sense. There are protests and questions. Soothing answers are provided by policy-makers and religious spokesmen are ready to support them with new adjustments. A new cycle is prepared. Once again there is a "just cause." Few stop to think that what is now regarded complacently as "justice" was clearly a crime twenty years ago.

How long can Christian morality go on taking this kind of beating?

There is only one winner in war. That winner is not justice, not liberty, not Christian truth.

The winner is war itself.

Peace: A Religious Responsibility

Between 1918 and 1939 religious opposition to war was articulate and widespread, all over Europe and America. Peace movements of significant proportions were active in Germany, Britain, and the United States. Yet they were crushed without difficulty and almost without protest by totalitarian regimes on the one hand, and silenced by the outbreak of a clearly defensive war on the other. Since 1945 there has been nothing to compare with the earlier movements of protest. Instead we have witnessed the enormous and crudely contrived fiction of the Communist Peace Movement which has been accepted with disillusioned resignation on one side of the Iron Curtain while, on the other, it has managed to make almost all efforts of independent civilian or religious groups to oppose nuclear war seem dishonest or subversive.

Yet never was opposition to war more urgent and more necessary than now. Never was religious protest so badly needed. Silence, passivity, or outright belligerence seem to be characteristic official and unofficial Christian reactions to the H-bomb. True, there has been some theological and ethical debate. This debate has been marked above all by a seemingly inordinate hesitation to characterize the uninhibited use of nuclear weapons as immoral. Of course the bomb has been condemned without equivocation by the "peace Churches" (Quakers, Mennonites, etc.). But the general tendency of Protestant and Catholic theologians has been to consider how far nuclear war could be reconciled with the traditional "just war" theory. In other words the discussion has been not so much a protest against nuclear war, still less a positive search for peaceful solutions to the problem of nuclear deterrence and ever increasing cold-war obsessions, but rather an attempt to justify, under some limited form, a new type of war which is tacitly recognized as an imminent possibility. This theological thought has tended more and more to *accept* the evil of nuclear war, considering it a lesser evil than Communist domination, and looking for some practicable way to make use of the lesser evil in order to avoid the greater.

But it would seem that a genuinely religious perspective, especially a Christian perspective, should be totally different. Therefore the purpose of the present article is to stand back from the imminent risks of the cold-war crisis, seeking to judge the problem of nuclear war not in relation to what seem to be our own interests or even our own survival, but simply in the light of moral truth. A Christian ought to consider whether nuclear war is not in itself a moral evil so great that it *cannot* be justified even for the best of ends, even to defend the highest and most sacrosanct of values.

This does not imply a purely pacifist rejection of war as such. Assuming that a "just war" is at least a theoretical possibility and granting that in a just war Christians may be bound to defend their country, the question we want to examine here is whether or not the massive and unlimited use of nuclear weapons, or the use of them in a limited first strike which is foreseen as likely to set off a global cataclysm, can be considered under any circumstances just.

The great problem is in fact that both in the East and in the West nuclear weapons are taken for granted. Nuclear war is now assumed to be a rational option or at least nuclear deterrence is accepted as a reasonable and workable way of "preserving peace." The moral issue is generally set aside as irrelevant. But if in all these cases a use of nuclear weapons even to threaten total or quasi-total destruction of an enemy is immoral, then we are living in a completely noxious situation where most of our political, economic, and even religious thinking is inseparably bound up with assumptions that may ultimately prove criminal. And if this is so, we must be prepared to face terrible consequences. For moral truth is not a sentimental luxury. It is as much a necessity to man and his society as air, water, fire, food and shelter.

This essay takes the stand that the *massive and uninhibited use of nuclear weapons,* either in attack or in retaliation, is contrary to Christian morality. And the arguments will be drawn particularly from Catholic sources. Recent Popes have declared ABC warfare (that is, atomic, biological and chemical warfare) to be a "sin, an offense and an outrage" (Pius XII). It may be quite true that these Popes have also affirmed a nation's right to defend itself by *just means,* in a *just war.* It may also be true that a theological argument for the use of "tactical nuclear weapons" may be constructed on the basis of some of the Popes' statements. But when we remember that the twenty kiloton A-bomb that was dropped on Hiroshima is now regarded as "small" and a "tactical device" and when we keep in mind that there is every probability that a force that is being beaten with small nuclear weapons will resort to big ones, we can easily see how little moral value can be found in these theorizings.

"Tactical nuclear weapons" and "limited war" with conventional forces are of course proposed with the best intentions: as a "realistic" way to avoid the horror of total nuclear warfare. Since it is claimed that men cannot get along without some kind of war, the least we can do is to insure that they will only destroy one another in thousands instead of in millions. Yet curiously enough, the restraint that would be required to keep within these limits (a restraint that was unknown on either side after the early phases of World War II), would seem to demand as much heroism and as much control as disarmament itself. It would therefore appear more realistic as well as more Christian and more humane to strive to think of total peace rather than of partial war. Why can we not do this? If disarmament were taken seriously, instead of being used as a pawn in the game of power politics, we could arrive at a workable agreement. It might not be ideal, but it would certainly be at once safer, saner and more realistic than war, whether limited or total. But we make ourselves incapable of taking either disarmament or peace with total seriousness, because we are completely obsessed with the fury and the fantasies of the cold war. The task of the Christian is to make the thought of peace once again seriously possible. A step towards this would be the rejection of nuclear deterrence as a basis for international policy. Nuclear war is totally unacceptable. It is immoral, inhuman, and absurd. It can lead nowhere but to the suicide of nations and of cultures, indeed to the destruction of human society itself.

We must now face the fact that we are moving closer and closer to war, not only as a result of blind social forces but also as the result of our own decisions and our own choice. The brutal reality is that, when all is said and done, we seem to *prefer* war; not that we want war itself, but we are blindly and hopelessly attached to all that makes war inevitable.

1 The Dance of Death

No one seriously doubts that it is now possible for man and his society to be completely destroyed in a nuclear war. This possibility must be soberly faced, even though it is so momentous in all its implications that we can hardly adjust ourselves to it in a fully rational manner. Indeed, this awful threat is the chief psychological weapon of the cold war. America and Russia are playing the paranoid game of nuclear deterrence, each one desperately hoping to preserve peace by threatening the other with bigger bombs and total annihilation.

Every step in this political dance of death brings us inexorably closer to hot war. The closer we get to hot war, the more the theoretical possibility of our total destruction turns into a real probability.

There is no control over the arbitrary and belligerent self-determination of the great nations ruled by managerial power elites concerned chiefly with their own self-interest. The UN is proving itself unable to fulfil the role of international arbiter and powerless to control the pugnacity of the nuclear club. Indeed, the big powers have been content to use the UN as a forum for political and propagandist wrestling matches and have not hesitated to take independent action that led to the discrediting of the UN whenever this has been profitable to them. Hence the danger that the uncontrolled power of nuclear weapons may break loose whenever one of the belligerents feels himself sufficiently strong and sufficiently provoked to risk an all-out war. Repeated threats to use the bomb have doubtless been mostly bluff, but one day somebody's bluff is going to be called, perhaps in a very drastic fashion.

Meanwhile the United States alone possesses a stockpile of nuclear weapons estimated at 60,000 megatons. This is enough to wipe out the present civilized world and to permanently affect all life on the planet earth. These nuclear bombs can be delivered by some 2,500 planes. It is no secret that such planes are constantly in the air, ready to strike. There are 200 missiles available to U.S. forces, mostly of intermediate range, and this does not suggest the immediate likelihood of a purely push-button war. But it is estimated that by 1963 there will be two thousand more of them, of which a large proportion will be intercontinental missiles based in "hard" installations. Attack on hard installations means ground bursts and therefore more fallout as well as more bombs. Hence even an attack concentrated on our missile bases is bound to have a destructive effect on many population centers.

An ICBM can carry an H-bomb warhead to a destination five thousand miles away, twenty times faster than the speed of sound. Intermediate-range missiles can be fired from submarines and deliver H-bombs which could reduce the eastern United States to a radioactive wasteland. H-bombs will soon be fitted to satellites and will be able to reach a target within a few minutes, without hope of interception.

It must be remembered that H-bombs are relatively cheap to produce, and it is not difficult to build and deliver big ones. Poison gas can also be delivered by long-range missiles. One such gas is manufactured in quantity by the U.S. Army Chemical Corps and it can exterminate whole populations of men as if they were insects. A similar nerve gas, originally developed by the Nazis, is manufactured in Soviet Russia. This gas is considered to be more effective against civilian populations than any nuclear agent. It leaves industry and property intact and there is no fallout! Shelters offer no protection against chemical agents.

In a word, the logic of deterrence has proved to be singularly illogical, because of the fact that nuclear war is almost exclusively offensive. So far there is no indication that there can be any really effective defense against guided missiles. All the advantage goes to the force that strikes first, without warning. Hence the multiplication of "hard" weapon sites, and of "deep shelters" becomes provocative and instead of convincing the enemy of our invulnerability, it only invites a heavier preemptive attack by bigger bombs and more of them. The cost of moving a significant portion of industry, business and the population underground is prohibitive and the whole idea is in itself nonsensical, at least as a guarantee of "peace."

Far from producing the promised "nuclear stalemate" and the "balance of terror" on which we are trying to construct an improbable peace, these policies simply generate tension, confusion, suspicion, and paranoid hate. This is the climate most suited to the growth of totalitarianism. Indeed, the cold war itself promises by itself to erode the last vestiges of true democratic freedom and responsibility even in the countries which claim to be defending these values. Those who think that they can preserve their independence, their civic and religious rights by ultimate recourse to the H-bomb do not seem to realize that the mere shadow of the bomb may end by reducing their religious and democratic beliefs to the level of mere words without meaning, veiling a state of rigid and totalitarian belligerency that will tolerate no opposition.

In a world where another Hitler and another Stalin are almost certain to appear on the scene, the existence of such destructive weapons and the moral paralysis of leaders and policy-makers combined with the passivity and confusion of mass societies which exist on both sides of the Iron Curtain, constitute the gravest problem in the whole history of man. Our times can be called apocalyptic, in the sense that we seem to have come to a point at which all the hidden, mysterious dynamism of the "history of salvation" revealed in the Bible has flowered into final and decisive crisis. The term "end of the world" may or may not be one that we are capable of understanding. But at any rate we seem to be assisting at the unwrapping of the mysteriously vivid symbols in the last book of the New Testament. In their nakedness they reveal to us our own selves as the men whose lot it is to live in a time of possibly ultimate decision. In a word, the end of our civilized society is quite literally up to us and to our immediate descendants, if any. It is for us to decide whether we are going to give in to hatred, terror and blind love of power for its own sake, and thus plunge our world into the abyss, or whether, restraining our savagery, we can patiently and humanely work together for interests which transcend the limits of any national or ideological community. We are challenged to prove we are rational, spiritual and humane enough to deserve survival, by acting according to the highest ethical and spiritual norms we know. As Christians, we believe that these norms have been given to us in the Gospel and in the traditional theology of the Church.

II The Christian as Peacemaker

We know that Christ came into this world as the Prince of Peace. We know that Christ Himself is our peace (Ephesians 2:14). We believe that God has chosen for Himself, in the Mystical Body of Christ, an elect people, regenerated by the Blood of the Savior, and committed by their baptismal promise to wage war upon the evil and hatred that are in man, and help to establish the Kingdom of God and of peace.

This means a recognition that human nature, identical in all men, was assumed by the Logos in the Incarnation, and that Christ died out of love for all men, in order to live in all men. Consequently we have the obligation to treat every other man as Christ Himself, respecting his life as if it were the life of Christ, his rights as if they were the rights of Christ. Even if the other shows himself to be unjust, wicked and odious to us, we cannot take upon ourselves a final and definitive judgment in his case. We still have an obligation to be patient, and to seek his highest spiritual interests. In other words, we are formally commanded to love our enemies, and this obligation cannot be met by a formula of words. It is not enough to press the button that will incinerate a city of five million people, saying in one's heart "this hurts me more than it hurts you," or declaring that it is all for love.

As Pope John XXIII pointed out in his first encyclical letter, *Ad Petri Cathedram,* Christians are obliged to strive for peace "with all the means at their disposal" and yet, as he continues, this peace cannot compromise with error or make concessions to it. Therefore it is by no means a matter of passive acquiescence in injustice, since this does not produce peace. However, the Christian struggle for peace depends first of all upon a free response of man to "God's call to the service of His Merciful designs" (Christmas message, 1958). Christ Our Lord did not come to bring peace to the world as a kind of spiritual tranquillizer. He brought to His disciples a vocation and a task, to struggle in the world of violence to establish His peace not only in their own hearts but in society itself. This was to be done not by wishing and fair words but by a total interior revolution in which we abandoned the human prudence that is subordinated to the quest for power, and followed the higher wisdom of love and of the Cross.

The Christian is and must be by his very adoption as a son of God, in Christ, a peacemaker (Matthew 5:9). He is bound to imitate the Savior who, instead of defending Himself with twelve legions of angels (Matthew 26:55), allowed Himself to be nailed to the Cross and died praying for His executioners. The Christian is one whose life has sprung from a particular spiritual seed: the blood of the martyrs who, without offering forcible resistance, laid down their lives rather than submit to the unjust laws that demanded an official religious cult of the emperor as God. That is to say, the Christian is bound, like the martyrs, to obey God rather than the state whenever the state tries to usurp powers that do not and cannot belong to it. We have repeatedly seen Christians in our time fulfilling this obligation in a heroic manner by their resistance to dictatorships that strove to interfere with the rights of their conscience and their religion.

Hence it must be stated quite clearly and without any compromise that the duty of the Christian as a peacemaker is not to be confused with a kind of quietistic inertia which is indifferent to injustice, accepts any kind of disorder, compromises with error and with evil, and gives in to every pressure in order to maintain "peace at any price." The Christian knows well, or should know well, that peace is not possible on such terms. Peace demands the most heroic labor and the most difficult sacrifice. It demands greater heroism than war. It demands greater fidelity to the truth and a much more perfect purity of conscience. The Christian fight for peace is not to be confused with defeatism. This has to be made clear because there is a certain complacent sophistry, given free currency by the theologians who want to justify war too easily, and who like to treat anyone who disagrees with them as if he were a practical apostate from the faith who had already surrendered implicitly to Communism by refusing to accept the morality of an all-out nuclear war. This, as any one can easily see, is simply begging the question. And one feels that those who yield to this temptation are perhaps a little too much influenced by the pragmatism and opportunism of our affluent society.

There is a lot of talk, among some of the clergy, about the relative danger of nuclear war and a "Communist takeover." It is assumed, quite gratuitously, that the Communist is at the gates, and is just about to take over the United States, close all the churches, and brainwash all the good Catholics. Once this spectral assessment of the situation is accepted, then one is urged to agree that there is only one solution: to let the Reds have it before they get our government and our universities thoroughly infiltrated. This means a preemptive strike, based not on the fact that we ourselves are actually under military attack, but that we are so "provoked" and so "threatened" that even the most drastic measures are justified.

If it is argued that there can be no proportion between the awful destruction wrought by nuclear war and the good achieved by exorcising this specter of Communist domination, the argument comes back: "better dead than Red." And this, in turn, is justified by the contention that the destruction of cities, nations, populations is "only a physical evil" while Communist domination would be a "moral evil."

It must be said at once that this has no basis in logic, ethics, politics or sound moral theology. Two quotations from Pope Pius XII will suffice to establish the true Catholic perspective on these points.

The destruction of cities and nations by nuclear war is "*only a physical evil?*" Pope Pius XII calls aggressive ABC warfare a "sin, an offense and an outrage against the majesty of God." And he adds: "It constitutes a crime worthy of the most severe national and international sanctions" (Address to the World Medical Congress, 1954). Fr. John Courtney Murray, S.J., whom no one can accuse of being a "pacifist" (he favors the licity of "limited nuclear war" and also believes that such a war would have practical value) has stated, "The extreme position of favoring a war . . . simply to kill off all Communists, cannot be a legitimate Catholic opinion."

The real issue here is not actually a moral principle so much as a state of mind. This state of mind is the one which we find in the American mass media. It is made up of a large number of very superficial assumptions about what is going on in the world and about what is likely to happen. We are in a sorry state, indeed, if our survival and indeed our Christian faith itself are left entirely at the mercy of such assumptions!

III   Beyond East and West

We are no longer living in a Christian world. The ages which we are pleased to call the "ages of faith" were certainly not ages of earthly paradise. But at least our forefathers officially recognized and favored the Christian ethic of love. They fought some very bloody and unchristian wars, and in doing so, they also committed great crimes which remain in history as a permanent scandal. However, certain definite limits were recognized. Today a non-Christian world still retains a few vestiges of Christian morality, a few formulas and clichés, which serve on appropriate occasions to adorn indignant editorials and speeches. But otherwise we witness deliberate campaigns to oppose and eliminate all education in Christian truth and morality. Not only non-Christians but even Christians themselves tend to dismiss the Gospel ethic of nonviolence and love as "sentimental." As a matter of fact, the mere suggestion that Christ counselled nonviolent resistance to evil is enough to invite scathing ridicule.

It is therefore a serious error to imagine that because the West was once largely Christian, the cause of the Western nations is now to be identified, without further qualification, with the cause of God. The incentive to wipe out Bolshevism with H-bombs may well be one of the apocalyptic temptations of twentieth-century Christendom. It may indeed be the most effective way of destroying Christendom, even though man may survive. For who imagines that the Asians and Africans will respect Christianity and receive it after it has apparently triggered mass murder and destruction of cosmic proportions? It is pure madness to think that Christianity can defend itself by nuclear preemption. The mere fact that we now seem to accept nuclear war as reasonable and Christian is a universal scandal.

True, Christianity is not only opposed to Communism, but in a very real sense, at war with it. However this warfare is spiritual and ideological. "Devoid of material weapons," says Pope John, "the Church is the trustee of the highest spiritual power." If the Church has no military weapons of her own, it means that her wars are fought without violence, not that she intends to call upon the weapons of nations that were once Christian, in defense of the Gospel. Whatever we may think of the ethics of nuclear war, it is clear that the message of the H-bomb is neither salvation nor "good news."

But we believe, precisely, that an essential part of the "good news" is that spiritual weapons are stronger than material ones. Indeed, by spiritual arms, the early Church conquered the entire Roman world. Have we lost our faith in this "sword of the Spirit?" Have we perhaps lost all realization of its very existence?

Of course we must repudiate a tactic of inert passivity that purely and simply leaves man defenseless, without any recourse whatever to any means of protecting himself, his rights, or Christian truth. We repeat again and again that the right, and truth, are to be defended by the most efficacious possible means, and that the most efficacious of all are precisely the spiritual ones, which have always been the only ones that have effected a really lasting moral change in society and in man. The Church tolerates defensive use of weapons only in so far as men are unable to measure up to the stricter and more heroic demands of spiritual warfare. It is absolutely unchristian to adopt, in practice, a standard of judgment which practically rejects or ignores all recourse to the spiritual weapons, and relegates them entirely to the background as if they had no efficacy whatever, and as if material weapons (the bigger the better) were the ones that really counted.

It seems that a great deal of the moral discussion about nuclear war is based, in fact, on the assumption that spiritual weapons are quixotic and worthless and that material weapons alone are worthy of serious consideration. But this attitude is precisely what leads to a fundamental vitiation of the Church's traditionally accepted doctrine on the use of violence in war: it seeks in every possible way to evade the obligation to use war only as a last resort, purely in *defense*, and with the use of *just means only*.

Inevitably, as soon as the obsession with bigger and bigger weapons takes hold of us, we make it impossible for ourselves to consider the just rights of noncombatants. We twist and deform the truth in every possible way in order to convince ourselves that noncombatants are really combatants after all, and that our "attack" is in reality "defense," while the enemy's "defense" really constitutes an "attack." By such tactics we disqualify ourselves from receiving the guidance of light and grace which will enable us to judge as spiritual men and as members of Christ. Obviously, without this special gift of light, we remain utterly incapable of seeing or appreciating the superiority of spiritual weapons, prayer, sacrifice, negotiation, and nonviolent means in general.

This results in the unhappy situation that non-Christians with rather dubious doctrinal support in irreligious philosophies have been able to take over characteristically Christian spiritual methods, appropriating them to themselves and thus further discrediting them in the eyes of the orthodox believer who is already confused by the now instinctive justification of war and weapons as the "normal" Christian way of solving international problems.

We must remember that the Church does not belong to any political power bloc. Christianity exists on both sides of the Iron Curtain and we should feel ourselves united by very special bonds with those Christians who, living under Communism, often suffer heroically for their principles.

Is it a valid defense of Christianity for us to wipe out those heroic Christians along with their oppressors, for the sake of "religious freedom"?

Let us stop and consider where the policy of massive retaliation and worse still of preemptive strike may lead us. Are we to annihilate huge population centers, at the same time showering vast areas around them with lethal fallout? Do we believe it is necessary to do this in order to protect ourselves against the menace of world Communism?

In these countries which we may perhaps be ready to annihilate, the vast majority is not Communist. On the contrary, while the people have resigned themselves passively to Communist domination, and have become quite convinced that there is no hope to be looked for from us because we are their declared enemies, and intend to wipe them out, they are by no means Communists. They do not want war. They have, in many cases, lived through the horrors and sacrifices of total war and experienced things which we are barely able to imagine. They do not want to go through this again.

We, in the name of liberty, of justice, of humanity, are pursuing a policy which promises to crush them with even greater horror, except that it may be perhaps "merciful" that millions of them will simply be blown out of existence in the twinkling of an eye. Merciful? When many of them have a Christian background, many are faithful Christians?

What good will our belligerent policy do us in those countries? None at all. It will only serve to reinforce the fatalistic conviction of the necessity of armament and of war that has been dinned into these populations by the Communist minority which dominates them.

How do we justify our readiness to wage a war of this kind? Let us face the fact that we feel ourselves terribly menaced by Communism. Certainly we believe we have to defend ourselves. Why are we menaced? Because, as time goes on, the Communists have gained a greater and greater advantage over us in the cold war. Why have they been able to do this? This is a question of historic fact, which, however, is not absolutely clear, but anyone will admit that our very reliance on the massive power of the bomb has to a great extent crippled us and restricted our freedom to maneuver, and the Communists have been operating under the *protection* of this massive threat that is too enormous to let loose for any but the most serious causes. Hence, instead of the serious provocation, the massive attack, we are confronted with a multiplicity of little threats all over the world, little advances, little gains. They all add up, but even the total of all of them does not constitute a sufficient reason for nuclear war.

But we are getting mad, and we are beginning to be thoroughly impatient with the humiliation of constant defeat. The more humiliated we become, the worse we compromise our chances, the greater errors we make.

We used to have an unrivaled reputation among the backward peoples of the world. We were considered the true defenders of liberty, justice and peace, the hope of the future. Our anger, our ignorance and our frustration have made us forfeit this tremendous advantage.

IV Moral Passivity and Demonic Activism

One of the most disturbing things about the Western world of our time is that it is beginning to have much more in common with the Communist world than it has with the professedly Christian society of several centuries ago. On both sides of the Iron Curtain we find two pathological varieties of the same moral sickness: both of them rooted in the same basically materialistic view of life. Both are basically opportunistic and pragmatic in their own way. And both have the following characteristics in common. On the level of *morality* they are blindly passive in their submission to a determination which, in effect, leaves men completely irresponsible. Therefore moral obligations and decisions tend to become practically meaningless. At best they are only forms of words, rationalizations of pragmatic decisions that have already been dictated by the needs of the moment.

Naturally, since not everyone is an unprincipled materialist even in Russia, there is bound to be some moral sense at work, even if only as a guilt-feeling that produces uneasiness and hesitation, blocking the smooth efficiency of machinelike obedience to immoral commands. Yet the history of Nazi Germany shows us how appalling was the irresponsibility which would carry out even the most revolting of crimes under cover of "obedience" to "legitimately constituted authority" for the sake of a "good cause." This moral passivity is the most terrible danger of our time, as the American bishops have already pointed out in their joint letters of 1960 and 1961.

On the level of political, economic and military activity, this moral passivity is balanced, or overbalanced by a *demonic activism*, a frenzy of the most varied, versatile, complex and even utterly brilliant technological improvisations, following one upon the other with an ever more bewildering and uncontrollable proliferation. Politics pretends to use this force as its servant, to harness it for social purposes, for the "good of man." The intention is good. The technological development of power in our time is certainly a risk and challenge, but it is by no means intrinsically evil. On the contrary, it can and should be a very great good. In actual fact, however, the furious speed with which our technological world is plunging toward disaster is evidence that no one is any longer fully in control—least of all, perhaps, the political leaders.

A simple study of the steps which led to the dropping of the first A-bomb on Hiroshima is devastating evidence of the way well-meaning men, the scientists, generals and statesmen of a victorious nation, were guided step by step, without realizing it, by the inscrutable yet simple "logic of events" to fire the shot that was to make the cold war inevitable and prepare the way inexorably for World War III. This they did purely and simply because they thought in all sincerity that the bomb was the simplest and most merciful way of ending World War II and perhaps all wars, forever.

The tragedy of our time is then not so much the malice of the wicked as the helpless futility of the best intentions of "the good." There are warmakers, war criminals, indeed. They are present and active on *both sides*. But all of us, in our very best efforts for peace, find ourselves maneuvered unconsciously into positions where we too can act as war criminals. For there can be no doubt that Hiroshima and Nagasaki were, though not fully deliberate crimes, nevertheless crimes. And who was responsible? No one. Or "history." We cannot go on playing with nuclear fire and shrugging off the results as "history." We are the ones concerned.

In plain words, in order to save ourselves from destruction we have to try to regain control of a world that is speeding downhill without brakes because of the combination of factors I have just mentioned: almost total passivity and irresponsibility on the moral level, plus demonic activism in social, political and military life.

First of all we must seek some remedy in the technological sphere. We must try to achieve some control over the production and stockpiling of weapons. It is intolerable that such massive engines of destruction should be allowed to proliferate in all directions without any semblance of a long-range plan for anything, even for what is cynically called "defense." To allow governments to pour more and more billions into weapons that almost immediately become obsolete, thereby necessitating more billions for newer and bigger weapons, is one of the most colossal injustices in the long history of man. While we are doing this, two thirds of the world are starving, or living in conditions of subhuman destitution.

Far from demanding that the lunatic race for destruction be stepped up, it seems to me that Christian morality imposes on every single one of us the obligation to protest against it and to work for the creation of an international authority with power and sanctions that will be able to control technology, and divert our amazing virtuosity into the service of man instead of against him.

It is not enough to say that we ought to try to work for a negotiated disarmament, or that one power bloc or the other ought to take the lead and disarm unilaterally. Methods and policies can and should be fairly considered. But what matters most is the obligation to travel in every feasible way in the direction of peace, using all the traditional and legitimate methods, while at the same time seeking to improvise new and original measures to achieve our end.

Long ago, even before the A-bomb, Pope Pius XII declared it was our supreme obligation to make "war on war" (1944). At that time he stressed our moral obligation to ban all wars of aggression, stating this duty was binding on *all* and that it "brooks no delay, no procrastination, no hesitation, no subterfuge." And what have we seen since then? The A-bomb, the H-bomb, the ICBM, the development of chemical and bacteriological weapons, and every possible evasion and subterfuge to justify their use without limitation as soon as one or the other nation decides that it may be expedient!

Therefore a Christian who is not willing to envisage the creation of an effective international authority to control the destinies of man for peace is not acting and thinking as a mature member of the Church. He does not have fully Christian perspectives. Such perspectives must, by their very nature, be "catholic," that is to say worldwide. They must consider the needs of mankind and not the temporary expediency and shortsighted policy of a particular nation.

To reject a "worldwide" outlook, to refuse to consider the good of mankind, and to remain satisfied with the affluence that flows from our war economy, is hardly a Christian attitude. Nor will our attachment to the current payoff accruing to us from weapons make it any easier for us to see and understand the need to take the hard road of sacrifice which alone leads to peace!

Equally important, and perhaps even more difficult than technological control, is the restoration of some moral sense and the resumption of genuine responsibility. Without this it is illusory for us to speak of freedom and "control." Unfortunately, even where moral principles are still regarded with some degree of respect, morality has lost touch with the realities of our situation. Modern warfare is fought as much by machines as by men. Even a great deal of the planning depends on the work of mechanical computers.

Hence it becomes more and more difficult to estimate the morality of an act leading to war because it is more and more difficult to know precisely what is going on. Not only is war increasingly a matter for pure specialists operating with fantastically complex machinery, but above all there is the question of absolute secrecy regarding everything that seriously affects defense policy. We may amuse ourselves by reading the reports in mass media and imagine that these "facts" provide sufficient basis for moral judgments for and against war. But in reality, we are simply elaborating moral fantasies in a vacuum. Whatever we may decide, we remain completely at the mercy of the governmental power, or rather the anonymous power of managers and generals who stand behind the facade of government. We have no way of directly influencing the decisions and policies taken by these people. In practice, we must fall back on a blinder and blinder faith which more and more resigns itself to trusting the "legitimately constituted authority" without having the vaguest notion what that authority is liable to do next. This condition of irresponsibility and passivity is extremely dangerous. It is hardly conducive to genuine morality.

An entirely new dimension is opened up by the fantastic processes and techniques involved in modern war. An American President can speak of warfare in outer space and nobody bursts out laughing—he is perfectly serious. Science fiction and the comic strip have all suddenly come true. When a missile armed with an H-bomb warhead is fired by the pressing of a button and its target is a whole city, the number of its victims is estimated in "megacorpses"—*millions* of dead human beings. A thousand or ten thousand more here and there are not even matter for comment. To what extent can we assume that the soldiers who exercise this terrible power are worthy of our confidence and actually realize what they are doing? To what extent can we assume that in passively following their lead and concurring in their decision—at least by default—we are acting as Christians?

V   *The Moral Problem*

In all-out nuclear war, there is no longer question of simply permitting an evil, the destruction of a few civilian dwellings, in order to attain a legitimate end: the destruction of a military target. It is well understood on both sides that all-out nuclear war is purely and simply massive and indiscriminate destruction of targets chosen not for their military significance alone, but for their importance in a calculated project of terror and annihilation. Often the selection of the target is determined by some quite secondary and accidental circumstance that has not the remotest reference to morality. Hiroshima was selected for atomic attack, among other reasons, because it had never undergone any notable air bombing and was suitable as an intact target to give a good idea of the effectiveness of the bomb.

It must be frankly admitted that some of the military commanders of both sides in World War II simply disregarded all the traditional standards that were still effective. The Germans threw those standards overboard with the bombs they unloaded on Warsaw, Rotterdam, Coventry and London. The Allies replied in kind with saturation bombing of Hamburg, Cologne, Dresden and Berlin. Spokesmen were not wanting on either side to justify these crimes against humanity. And today, while "experts" calmly discuss the possibility of the United States being able to survive a war if "*only fifty millions*" (!) of the population are killed, when the Chinese speak of being able to *spare* "three hundred million" and "still get along," it is obvious that we are no longer in the realm where moral truth is conceivable.

The only sane course that remains is to work frankly and without compromise for a supranational authority and for the total abolition of war. The pronouncements of the Holy See all seem to point to this as the best ultimate solution.

The moral duty of the Christian is by no means simple. It is far from being a neat matter of ethical principle, clear cut, well defined, and backed by a lucid authoritative decision of the Church. To make the issue seem too simple is actually to do a great disservice to truth, to morality and to man. And yet now more than ever we crave the simple and the clear solution. This very craving is dangerous, because the most tempting of all "simple" solutions are the ones which prescribe annihilation or submit to it without resistance. There is a grim joke underlying all this talk about "Red or dead." The inherent destructiveness of the frustrated mind is able to creep in here and distort the whole Christian view of life and of civilization by evading the difficult and complex way of negotiation and sacrifice, in order to resort, in frustrated desperation, to "magic" power and nuclear destruction. Let us not ignore this temptation, it is one of the deepest and most radical in man. It is the first of all temptations, and the root of all the others. "You shall be as gods. . . ." (Genesis 3:5).

On the contrary, our Christian obligation consists in being and remaining men, believing in the Word Who emptied Himself and became man for our sakes. We have to look at the problem of nuclear war from the viewpoint of humanity and of God made man, from the viewpoint of the Mystical Body of Christ, and not merely from the viewpoint of abstract formulas. Here above all we need a reasoning that is informed with compassion and takes some account of flesh and blood, not a legalistic juggling with principles and precedents.

In the light of these deep Christian truths we will better understand the danger of fallacious justifications of every recourse to violence, as well as the peril of indifference, inertia and passivity.

It is not a question of stating absolutely and infallibly that every Christian must renounce, under pain of mortal sin, any opinion that the use of the bomb might be legitimate. The H-bomb has not been formally and officially condemned, and doubtless it does not need to be condemned. There is no special point in condemning one weapon in order to give casuistical minds an opportunity to prove their skill in evasion by coming up with another, "licit" way of attaining the same destructive end. It is not just a matter of seeing how much destruction and murder we can justify without incurring the condemnation of the Church.

But I submit that at this time above all it is vitally important to avoid the "minimalist" approach. The issue of nuclear war is too grave and too general. It threatens everybody. It may affect the very survival of the human race. In such a case one is not allowed to take any but unavoidable risks. We are obliged to take the morally more secure alternative in guiding our choice. Let us remember too that while a doubt of the existence of an obligation leaves us with a certain freedom of choice, the doubt of an evil fact does not permit such freedom.

We may well dispute the legitimacy of nuclear war on principle: but when we face the *actual fact* that recourse to nuclear weapons may quite probably result in the quasi-total destruction of civilization, even possibly in the suicide of the entire human race, we *are absolutely obliged to take this fact into account and to avoid this terrible danger.*

It is certainly legitimate for a Catholic moralist to hold in theory that a limited nuclear war, in defense, is permitted by traditional Christian moral principles. He may even hold the opinion that the strategic use of nuclear, bacteriological and chemical weapons is theoretically permissible for defense, provided that there is a possibility that what we are defending will continue to exist after it has been "defended."

But when we come face to face with the terrible doubt of fact, *dubium facti,* the absolutely real and imminent probability of massive and uncontrolled destruction with the annihilation of civilization and of life, then there is no such latitude of choice. We are most gravely and seriously bound by all norms of Christian morality, however minimal, to choose the safer course and to try at all costs to avoid so general a disaster.

Let us remember that even if one were to admit the theoretical legitimacy of nuclear weapons for purposes of defense, that use would become gravely unjust, without a shadow of doubt, as soon as the effects of nuclear destruction overflowed upon neutral or friendly nations. Even though we may feel justified in risking the destruction of our own cities and those of the enemy, we have no right whatever to bring destruction upon helpless small nations which have no interest whatever in the war and ask only to survive in peace. It is not up to us to choose that *they* should be dead rather than Red.

Pope Pius XII said in 1954 (concerning ABC warfare, described above as a sin, an offense and an outrage against God): "Should the evil consequences of adopting this method of warfare *ever become so extensive as to pass entirely beyond the control of man, then indeed its use must be rejected as immoral.*" He adds that uncontrolled annihilation of life within a given area "IS NOT LAWFUL UNDER ANY TITLE."

Nor is it moral to overindulge in speculation on this dangerous point of "control." A lax interpretation of this principle would lead us to decide that a twenty megaton H-bomb dropped on Leningrad is "fully under control" because all its effects are susceptible to measurement, and we know that the blast will annihilate Leningrad while the fallout will probably wipe out the population of Helsinki and Riga, depending on the wind. Obviously what the Pope meant was much more strict than that. He meant that if there was uncontrolled annihilation of everybody in Leningrad, without any discrimination between combatants and noncombatants, enemies, friends, women, children, infants and old people, then the use of the bomb would be "not lawful under any title," especially in view of the "bonus" effects of fallout drifting over neutral territory, certainly without control. And I do not think "clean" bombs are going to get around this moral difficulty either.

Hence though nuclear warfare as such has not been entirely and formally condemned, the mind of the Church is obviously that every possible means should be taken to avoid it; and John XXIII made this abundantly clear in his Christmas Message of 1961 where he pleaded in most solemn terms with the rulers of all nations to "shun all thought of force" and remain at peace. The words of Pope John in this connection imply grave reservations even with regard to limited war which might possibly "escalate" and reach all-out proportions.

There can be no doubt whatever that the absence of formal condemnation cannot be twisted into a tacit official approval of all-out nuclear war. Yet it seems that this is what some of our theologians are trying to do.

On the contrary, out duty is to help emphasize with all the force at our disposal that the Church earnestly seeks the abolition of war; we must underscore declarations like those of Pope John XXIII pleading with world leaders to renounce force in the settlement of international disputes and confine themselves to negotiations.

Now let us suppose that the political leaders of the world, supported by the mass media in their various countries, and carried on by a tidal wave of greater and greater war preparations, see themselves swept inexorably into a war of cataclysmic proportions. Let us suppose that it becomes morally certain that these leaders are helpless to arrest the blind force of the process that has irresponsibly been set in motion. What then? Are the masses of the world, including you and me, to resign themselves to our fate and march to global suicide without resistance, simply bowing our heads and obeying our leaders as showing us the "will of God?" I think it should be evident to everyone that this can no longer, in the present situation, be accepted unequivocally as Christian obedience and civic duty.

It is true that Pope Pius XII in his Christmas Message of 1956 declared that a Catholic was bound in duty to help his country in a just war of defense. But to extend this to all-out nuclear war is begging the question because Papal pronouncements on nuclear war cast doubts upon its justice. No theologian, however broad, however lax, would insist that one was bound in conscience to participate in a war that was *evidently* leading to global suicide. Those who favor nuclear war can only do so by making all kinds of suppositions concerning the political and military facts: that it will be only a limited war or that the destructive effects of H-bombs are not as terrible as we have been told. However much they limit the scoresheet of mega-corpses, it is difficult for us to admit the morality of all-out nuclear war.

This brings us face to face with the greatest and most agonizing moral issue of our time. This issue is not merely nuclear war, not merely the possible destruction of the human race by a sudden explosion of violence. It is something more subtle and more demonic.

If we continue to yield to theoretically irresistible determinism and to vague "historic forces" without striving to resist and control them, if we let these forces drive us to demonic activism in the realm of politics and technology, we face something more than the material evil of universal destruction. We face *moral responsibility for global suicide*. Much more than that, we are going to find ourselves gradually moving into a situation in which we are practically compelled by the "logic of circumstances" deliberately *to choose the course that leads to destruction*.

The great danger is then the savage and self-destructive commitment to a policy of nationalism and blind hate, and the refusal of all other policies more constructive and more in accordance with Christian ethical tradition. Let us realize that this is a matter of *choice*, not of pure blind determinism.

We all know the logic of temptation. We all know the confused, vague, hesitant irresponsibility which leads us into the situation where it is no longer possible to turn back, and how, arrived in that situation, we have a moment of clear-sighted desperation in which we freely commit ourselves to the course we recognize as evil. That may well be what is happening now to the whole world.

The free choice of global suicide, made in desperation by the world's leaders and ratified by the consent and cooperation of their citizens, would be a moral evil second only to the Crucifixion. The fact that such a choice might be made with the highest motives and the most urgent purpose would do nothing whatever to mitigate it. The fact that it might be made as a gamble, in the hope that some might escape, would never excuse it. After all, the purposes of Caiphas were, in his own eyes, perfectly noble. He thought it was necessary to let "one man die for the people."

The most urgent necessity of our time is therefore not merely to prevent the destruction of the human race by nuclear war. Even if it should happen to be no longer possible to prevent the disaster (which God forbid), there is still a greater evil than can and must be prevented. It must be possible for every free man to refuse his consent and deny his cooperation to this greatest of crimes.

VI   *The Christian Choice*

In what does this effective and manifest refusal of consent consist? How does one "resist" the sin of genocide? Ideally speaking, in the imaginary case where all-out nuclear war seemed inevitable and the world's leaders were evidently incapable of preventing it, it would be legitimate and even obligatory for all sane and conscientious men everywhere in the world to lay down their weapons and their tools and starve and be shot rather than cooperate in the war effort. If such a mass movement should spontaneously arise in all parts of the world, in Russia and America, in China and France, in Africa and Germany, the human race could be saved from extinction. This is indeed an engaging hypothesis—but it is no more than that. It would be folly to suppose that men hitherto passive, inert, morally indifferent and irresponsible might suddenly recover their sense of obligation and their awareness of their own power when the world was on the very brink of war.

In any case, as has been said above, the ordinary man has no access to vital information. Indeed, even the politicians may know relatively little about what is really going on. How would it be possible to know when and how it was necessary to refuse cooperation? Can we draw a line clearly, and say precisely when nuclear war becomes so dangerous that it is suicidal? If a war of missiles breaks out, we will have at the most thirty minutes to come to our momentous conclusions —if we ever know what is happening at all. It seems to me that the time to form our conscience and to decide upon our course of action is NOW.

It is one thing to form one's conscience and another to adopt a specific policy or course of action. It is highly regrettable that this important distinction is overlooked and indeed deliberately obfuscated. To decide, in the forum of conscience, that one is obligated in every way, as a Christian, to avoid actions that would contribute to a world-wide disaster, does not mean that one is necessarily committed to absolute and unqualified pacifism. One may start from this moral principle, which is repeatedly set before us by the Popes and which cannot be seriously challenged, and one may then go on to seek various means to preserve peace. About these different means, there may be considerable debate.

Yet it seems clear to me that the enormous danger represented by nuclear weapons, and the near impossibility of controlling them and limiting them to a scale that would fit the traditional ethical theory of a just war, makes it both logical and licit for a Catholic to proceed, from motives of conscience, to at least a relative pacifism, and to a policy of nuclear disarmament.

In so doing, however, he has a strict obligation to see that he does not take a naïve and oversimplified position which would permit him to be ruthlessly exploited by the politicians of another nuclear power. The logic of all serious efforts to preserve peace demands that our very endeavors themselves do not help the war effort of the "enemy," and thus precipitate war. There is sometimes a danger that our pacifism may be somewhat shortsighted and immature. It may consequently be more an expression of rebellion against the status quo in our own country than an effective opposition to war itself.

In a word, there are three things to be considered: (1) Christian moral principles, which by their very nature favor peace, and according to which nuclear war remains, if not absolutely forbidden, at least of exceedingly dubious morality; (2) The facts about weapons systems and defense policies. Our moral decision, and the morality of our participation in the economic and political life of a society geared for nuclear war, demand imperatively that we realize the real nature of the military policies to which we contribute by taxation and perhaps also by our work in industry. So much in our national life is today centered on the most intense and most overwhelming arms race in the history of man. Everything points to the fact that these frightful weapons of destruction may soon be used, most probably on the highest and most expanded scale; (3) We must finally consider factors by which these military policies are dictated.

The Christian moral principles are relatively clear. While there is still intense debate over details, no Christian moralist worthy of the name can seriously defend outright a nuclear war of unqualified aggression.

The facts about ABC warfare are also clear enough. There is no question of the immense destructiveness of the weapons available to us. There is no question that the destruction of civilization and even global suicide are both possible. There is no question that the policies of the nuclear powers are geared for an all-out war of incredible savagery and destructive force.

What remains to be explored by the Christian is the area that is least considered, which also happens to be the area that most needs to be examined and is perhaps the one place where something can be done.

By what are our policies of hatred and destructiveness dictated? What seems to drive us inexorably on to the fate which we all dread and seek to avoid? This question is not hard to answer. What started the First World War? What started the Second World War? The answer is, simply, the rabid, shortsighted, irrational and stubborn forces which tend to come to a head in nationalism.

Christopher Dawson has said:

> The defeat of Hitlerism does not mean that we have seen the end of such movements. In our modern democratic world, irrational forces lie very near the surface, and *their sudden eruption under the impulse of nationalist or revolutionary ideologies is the greatest of all the dangers that threaten the modern world.* . . . It is at this point that the need for a reassertion of Christian principles becomes evident. In so far as nationalism denies the principle (of higher order and divine justice for all men) and sets up the nation and the national state as the final object of man's allegiance, *it represents the most retrograde movement the world has ever seen,* since it means a denial of the great central truth on which civilization

was founded, and the return to the pagan idolatries of tribal barbarism.

Dawson then goes on to quote Pope Pius XII who distinguishes between "national life" and "nationalistic politics." National life is a combination of all the values which characterize a social group and enable it to contribute fruitfully to the whole policy of nations. Nationalistic politics on the other hand are divisive, destructive, and a perversion of genuine national values. They are "a principle of dissolution within the community of peoples."

This then is the conclusion: the Christian is bound to work for peace by working against global dissolution and anarchy. Due to nationalist and revolutionary ideologies (for Communism is in fact exploiting the intense nationalism of backward peoples), a world-wide spirit of confusion and disorder is breaking up the unity and the order of civilized society.

It is true that we live in an epoch of revolution, and that the breakup and re-formation of society is inevitable. But the Christian must see that his mission is not to contribute to the blind forces of annihilation which tend to destroy civilization and mankind together. He must seek to build rather than to destroy. He must orient his efforts towards world unity and not towards world division. Anyone who promotes policies of hatred and of war is working for the division and the destruction of civilized mankind.

We have to be convinced that there are certain things already clearly forbidden to all men, such as the use of torture, the killing of hostages, genocide (or the mass extermination of racial, national or other groups for no reason than that they belong to an "undesirable" category). The destruction of civilized centers by nuclear annihilation bombing is genocide.

We have to become aware of the poisonous effect of the mass media that keep violence, cruelty and sadism constantly present to the minds of unformed and irresponsible people. We have to recognize the danger to the whole world in the fact that today the economic life of the more highly-developed nations is in large part centered on the production of weapons, missiles and other engines of destruction.

We have to consider that the hate propaganda, and the consistent heckling of one government by another, has always inevitably led to violent conflict. We have to recognize the implications of voting for politicians who promote policies of hate. We must never forget that our most ordinary decisions may have terrible consequences.

It is no longer reasonable or right to leave all decisions to a largely anonymous power elite that is driving us all, in our passivity, towards ruin. We have to make ourselves heard.

Every individual Christian has a grave responsibility to protest clearly and forcibly against trends that lead inevitably to crimes which the Church deplores and condemns. Ambiguity, hesitation and compromise are no longer permissible. We must find some new and constructive way of settling international disputes. This may be extraordinarily difficult. Obviously war cannot be abolished by mere wishing. Severe sacrifices may be demanded and the results will hardly be visible in our day. We have still time to do something about it, but the time is rapidly running out.

An Enemy of the State

On August 9, 1943, the Austrian peasant Franz Jägerstätter was be-
headed by the German military authorities as an "enemy of the state"
because he had repeatedly refused to take the military oath and serve
in what he declared to be an "unjust war." His story has a very special
importance at a time when the Catholic Church, in the Second Vatican
Council, is confronting the moral problem of nuclear weaponry. This
Austrian peasant was not only simultaneously a Catholic and a conscientious objector, but he was a fervent Catholic, so fervent that some
who knew him believe him to have been a saint. His lucid and un-
compromising refusal to fight for Germany in the Second World War
was the direct outcome of his religious conversion. It was the political
implementation of his desire to be a perfect Christian.

Franz Jägerstätter surrendered his life rather than take the lives of
others in what he believed to be an "unjust war." He clung to this belief in the face of every possible objection not only on the part of the
army and the state, but also from his fellow Catholics, the Catholic
clergy and of course his own family. He had to meet practically every
"Christian" argument that is advanced in favor of war. He was treated
as a rebel, disobedient to lawful authority, a traitor to his country. He
was accused of being selfish, self-willed, not considering his family,
neglecting his duty to his children.

His Austrian Catholic friends understood that he was unwilling to
fight for Hitler's Germany, but yet they argued that the war was justified because they hoped it would lead to the destruction of Bolshevism
and therefore to the preservation of "European Christianity." He was
therefore refusing to defend his faith. He was also told that he was not
sufficiently informed to judge whether or not the war was just. That he
had an obligation to submit to the "higher wisdom" of the state. The
government and the Fuehrer know best. Thousands of Catholics, including many priests, were serving in the armies, and therefore he
should not try to be "more Catholic than the Church."

He was even reminded that the bishops had not protested against this war, and in fact not only his pastor but even his bishop tried to persuade him to give up his resistance because it was "futile." One priest represented to him that he would have innumerable opportunities to practice Christian virtue and exercise an "apostolate of good example" in the armed forces. All these are very familiar arguments frequently met with in our present situation, and they are still assumed to be so conclusive that few Catholics dare to risk the disapproval they would incur by conscientious objection and dissent.

Jäggerstätter's fellow villagers thought his refusal was evidence of fanaticism due to his religious conversion at the time of his marriage in 1936, followed by an "excess of Bible reading." His conscientious objection is still not fully understood in his native village, though on the local war memorial his name has been added to those of the villagers who were killed in action.

The peasant refused to give in to any of these arguments, and replied to them with all simplicity:

> I cannot and may not take an oath in favor of a government that is fighting an unjust war. . . . I cannot turn the responsibility for my actions over to the Führer. . . . Does anyone really think that this massive blood-letting can save European Christianity or bring it to a new flowering? . . . Is it not more Christian to offer oneself as a victim right away rather than first have to murder others who certainly have a right to live and want to live—just to prolong one's own life a little while?

When reminded that most Catholics had gone to war for Hitler without any such qualms of conscience, he replied that they obviously "had not received the grace" to see things as they were. When told that the bishops themselves expressed no such objections he repeated that "they had not received the grace" either.

Jägerstätter's refusal to fight for Hitler was not based on a personal repugnance to fighting in any form. As a matter of fact Jägerstätter was, by temperament, something of a fighter. In his wilder youthful days he had participated rather prominently in the inter-village gang wars. He had also undergone preliminary military training without protest, though his experience at that time had convinced him that army life presented a danger to morals.

Shortly after Hitler took over Austria in 1938, Jägerstätter had a dream in which he saw a splendid and shining express train coming round a mountain, and thousands of people running to get aboard. "No one could prevent them from getting on the train." While he was looking at this he heard a voice saying: "This train is going to hell." When he woke up he spontaneously associated the "train" with Nazism. His objection to military service was, then, the fruit of a particular religious interpretation of contemporary political events. His refusal to fight was not only a private matter of conscience: it also expressed a

deep intuition concerning the historical predicament of the Catholic
Church in the twentieth century. This intuition was articulated in several long and very impressive meditations or "commentaries" in which
he says:

> The situation in which we Christians of Germany find ourselves
> today is much more bewildering than that faced by the Chris-
> tians of the early centuries at the time of their bloodiest perse-
> cution. . . . We are not dealing with a small matter, but the
> great (apocalyptic) life and death struggle has already begun.
> Yet in the midst of it there are many who still go on living their
> lives as though nothing had changed. . . . That we Catholics
> must make ourselves tools of the worst and most dangerous anti-
> Christian power that has ever existed is something that I cannot
> and never will believe. . . . Many actually believe quite simply
> that things have to be the way they are. If this should happen
> to mean that they are obliged to commit injustice, then they
> believe that others are responsible. . . . I am convinced that
> it is still best that I speak the truth even though it costs me my
> life. For you will not find it written in any of the command-
> ments of God or of the Church that a man is obliged under pain
> of sin to take an oath committing him to obey whatever might
> be commanded him by his secular ruler. We need no rifles or
> pistols for our battle, but instead spiritual weapons—and the
> foremost of these is prayer.

The witness of this Austrian peasant is in striking contrast to the
career of another man who lived and worked for a time in the nearby
city of Linz: Adolf Eichmann.

The American sociologist Gordon Zahn, who is also a Catholic and
a pacifist, has written an absorbing, objective, fully documented life
of Jäggerstätter,[1] in which he studies with great care not only the
motives and actions of the man himself, but the reactions and recollec-
tions of scores of people who knew him, from his family and neighbors
to fellow prisoners and prison chaplains. One of the most striking things
about the story is that repeated attempts were made to save the
peasant-objector's life not only by his friends, by priests, by his attorney
but even by his military judges (he was not in the hands of the SS).

Jäggerstätter could have escaped execution if he had accepted noncombatant service in the medical corps, but he felt that even this would
be a compromise, because his objection was not only to killing other
men but to the act of saving his own life by an implicit admission that
the Nazis were a legitimate regime carrying on a just war. A few minutes before his execution Jägerstätter still calmly refused to sign a
document that would have saved him. The chaplain who was present,

1. *In Solitary Witness* (New York: Holt, Rinehart & Winston, 1964).

and who had tried like everyone else to persuade the prisoner to save himself, declared that Jägerstätter "lived as a saint and died as a hero."

It is important to observe that though the Catholic villagers of his native St. Radegund still tend to regard Jägerstätter as an extremist and a fanatic, or even as slightly touched in the head, the priests who knew him and others who have studied him have begun to admit the seriousness and supernatural impact of his heroic self-sacrifice. There are some who do not hesitate to compare his decision with that of Thomas More.

One of the prison chaplains who knew him said: "Not for an instant did I ever entertain the notion that Jägerstätter was 'fanatic' or even possibly mentally deranged. He did not give the slightest impression of being so." And a French cellmate said of him that he was "one of the heroes of our time, a fighter to the death for faith, peace and justice."

Finally, it is interesting to read the very reserved judgment of the bishop who, when consulted by Jägerstätter about this moral problem, urged him to renounce his "scruples" and let himself be inducted into the army.

> I am aware of the "consistency" of his conclusions and respect them—especially in their intention. At that time I could see that the man thirsted after martyrdom and for the expiation of sin, and I told him that he was permitted to choose that path only if he knew he had been called to it through some special revelation originating from above and not in himself. He agreed with this. For this reason Jägerstätter represents a completely exceptional case, one more to be marveled at than copied.

The story of the Austrian peasant as told by Gordon Zahn is plainly that of a martyr, and of a Christian who followed a path of virtue with a dedication that cannot be fully accounted for by human motivation alone. In other words, it would seem that already in this biography one might find plausible evidence of what the Catholic Church regards as sanctity. But the Bishop of Linz, in hinting at the possibility of a special calling that might have made Jägerstätter an "exceptional case," does not mean even implicitly to approve the thesis that the man was a saint, still less a model to be imitated. In other words the bishop, while admitting the remote possibility of Catholic heroism in a conscientious objector, is not admitting that such heroism should be regarded as either normal or imitable.

The Second Vatican Council in its Constitution on the Church in the Modern World (n. 79) recognized, at least implicitly, the right of a Catholic to refuse on grounds of conscience to bear arms. It did not propose conscientious objection as a sweeping obligation. Nevertheless it clearly declared that no one could escape the obligation to *refuse obedience* to criminal orders issued by the state or the military command. The example of genocide was given. In view of the fact that total war tends more and more in fact to be genocidal, the Council's declaration obviously bears above all on war.

The Bishop of Linz, however, did not propose conscientious objection as a rational and Christian option. For him, the true heroes remain "those exemplary young Catholic men, seminarians, priests and heads of families who fought and died in heroic fulfillment of duty and in the firm conviction that they were fulfilling the will of God at their post. . . ."

It is still quite possible that even today after the Council and in an era of new war technology and new threats of global destruction, when the most urgent single problem facing modern man is the proliferation of atomic and nuclear weaponry, many Catholic bishops will continue to agree with this one. It is true, they admit that there is such a thing as an erroneous conscience which is to be followed provided it is "invincible." "All respect is due to the innocently erroneous conscience," says the Bishop of Linz, "it will have its reward from God."

Of whom is he speaking? Of the Catholic young men, the priests and the seminarians who died in Hitler's armies "in the firm conviction that they were fulfilling the will of God"? No. These, he says, were men (and the word is underlined) acting in the light of "a clear and correct conscience." Jägerstätter was "in error" but also "in good faith."

Certainly the bishop is entitled to his opinion: but the question of whose conscience was erroneous and whose was correct remains one that will ultimately be settled by God, not man. Meanwhile there is another question: the responsibility of those who help men to form their conscience—or fail to do so. And here, too, the possibility of firm convictions that are "innocently erroneous" gives food for some rather apocalyptic thought.

The real question raised by the Jägerstätter story is not merely that of the individual Catholic's right to conscientious objection (admitted in practice even by those who completely disagreed with Jägerstätter) but the question of the Church's own mission of protest and prophecy in the gravest spiritual crisis man has ever known.

A Martyr for Peace and Unity:

Father Max Josef Metzger
(1887-1944)

Once again the civilized world sways on the brink of an abyss. This time the abyss seems to be bottomless. Once again the passions and confusions of social life have cruelly obscured the great problem of conscience that faces Christians in the twentieth century; that has, indeed, faced them for centuries. The problem of dissension, division and war. The Christian duty to fight for peace and unity.

Once again we confront the confusion between the obligation to respond without compromise to the Law of Christ, the Law of Peace, and the apparent duty to give first place to the warlike demands of the power politician. As Pope John XXIII has said in his Christmas Message of 1961: "All the teaching of Christ is an invitation to peace, for it proclaims the blessedness of peace. But (in politics) under the cloak of fair words, there is often a spirit opposed to peace." As we know, the great power blocs stand armed for mutual annihilation, each one claiming to be the only defender of "peace." Let us hope that the appeal of Pope John to "those responsible for forming public opinion" and to "the rulers of nations who hold in their hands the fate of mankind" may at last be heeded. He asks the propagandist in particular to "fear the severe judgment of God and to proceed with caution, governed by a sense of balance" instead of fomenting hatred among nations and races. Catholics at least are seriously bound in conscience to listen to this solemn warning of the Vicar of Christ, regarding hate propaganda and incitement to war, no matter how "good" the apparent cause may be.

When Hitler finally plunged the Western world into war by his attack on Poland, the German Catholics, and especially the German Catholic press, feeling that their duty was first of all to support

Reich und Volk, followed Hitler into battle without complaint. The Catholic who might perhaps have suffered from some pangs of conscience was officially reassured that this was a perfectly "just war." We who are far removed from the scene can judge the situation with critical and perhaps severe detachment. We can see, for instance, for what understandable reasons the German Catholic press at that time wanted to continue in existence and supported Hitler's war effort in order to avoid immediate suppression. We forget that here and there in the columns of Catholic papers and magazines were items which said much to those who knew how to read between the lines, and which could hardly be published without heroism on the part of those who knew how closely their proofs were scrutinized by the Gestapo.

And yet the lesson is inescapable in its tragic implications. In the modern godless world, where a heroic choice may be demanded, where peace and even the survival of mankind may conceivably depend on such a choice being made by Christians, we can blind our own conscience with a false conception of duty and of sacrifice which enables us quietly to participate in colossal injustices and barbarities, in order to preserve our institutional freedom of action. It is so easy to fear men more than God, so easy to feel that social ostracism is a greater danger than infidelity to conscience and to Christ. All our economic interests are there to persuade us that the side of God is the side on which our bread happens to be buttered. This does not imply that our moral obligations are always clear. But when such tremendous issues confront us, let us at least realize our moral risk. Let us at least consider that our obligation to Christ the King takes precedence over every other obligation. We must beware of seeing in our duties to Caesar a sweeping justification for cruelty, moral cowardice, infidelity, greed, and what Pope John has called the "callousness of the complacent man who pays no heed to the great cry of suffering which exists in the world."

The example of Max Josef Metzger, a Catholic priest executed by Hitler's Gestapo in the Brandenburg Prison, Berlin, on April 17, 1944, should make us realize that not everyone needs to be a passive utensil of the militarist. Father Metzger was a true patriot. He never failed his country, even though in Hitler's eyes he was a "traitor to the Reich and Führer." He died for Germany just as heroically and just as wholeheartedly as any soldier who fell on the battlefield. And he died for peace. It was indeed his attempts to work out a plan for peace in conjunction with bishops in other countries that was regarded by Hitler as "treason."

Father Metzger had been a chaplain in World War I. He had revolted against the senseless horrors of a war that achieved nothing, that only brought about moral and physical destruction and prepared the way for a still greater cataclysm.

Right after World War I he became a devoted worker in the

cause of peace. He was in contact with the International Fellowship of Reconciliation. He attended many peace conferences and congresses and founded a Secular Institute, the Society of Christ the King, devoted to the lay apostolate and works of mercy, particularly to work in the cause of international peace. He was also ardently devoted to the cause of Christian unity. He was, with Abbé Courturier in France, one of the most original and farsighted precursors of the present flourishing Catholic ecumenical movement. The best-known work of Father Metzger is the *Una Sancta* movement which began in 1939 with the retreat of a group of Catholic and Protestant clergymen, together, in search of a basis for agreement and fraternal union that would remotely prepare the way for Christian Unity. *Una Sancta* is today one of the most lively and flourishing of Catholic ecumenical endeavors.

Father Metzger was arrested three times before his last imprisonment which ended with his execution. He was jailed by the Gestapo in 1934, 1938, 1939 and finally in 1943. The first three prison terms involved sedulous examination of Father Metzger, in an effort to pin some kind of charge on him, and especially to implicate him in a conspiracy against the Führer. He was not engaged in any such conspiracy.

What finally emerged as "treason" sufficient to warrant a death sentence was his sincere, almost naïve effort to get a peace plan going which he thought would end the war. Through the intermediary of a Swedish woman, who was interested in *Una Sancta,* Father Metzger wanted to get letters out of Germany to bishops in various warring and neutral countries. He thought that the bishops would be able to influence their governments to seek a negotiated peace instead of the "unconditional surrender" that was to cost Germany so many burned and gutted cities, so many thousands of civilian dead. The Swedish lady was a Gestapo agent. The letters of Father Metzger, suggesting as they did that Germany needed to be "spared" and that the Reich would not come back to destroy all her enemies, was of course regarded as treason by Hitler.

Let us remember this formula: in the madness of modern war, when every crime is justified, the nation is always right, power is always right, the military is always right. To question those who wield power, to differ from them in any way, is to confess oneself subversive, rebellious, traitors. Father Metzger did not believe in power, in bombs. He believed in Christ, in unity, in peace. He died as a martyr for his belief.

Words of Father Metzger

1. I HAVE OPENED MY LIPS FOR THE PEACE OF THE WORLD AND THE UNITY OF CHRIST'S CHURCH. GOD HAS ACCEPTED IT AND I AM GLAD.

2. War owes its existence to the Father of lies. War is itself a lie. War is the kingdom of Satan, Peace is the Kingdom of God. The "just war" of which the moralists wrote in former days is now no longer possible. War today is a crime. We need to organize peace as men have organized war. Men of all peoples and nations, unite against the inhuman thing and declare that you will have no part in it, neither by taking up arms nor by transporting war materials nor in any other way.

3. IT IS HONORABLE TO DIE FOR ONE'S COUNTRY BUT STILL MORE HONORABLE TO DIE FOR RIGHTEOUSNESS AND PEACE.

4. Strive after love, strive unwearily after love, the selfless love that is ready for sacrifice.

5. God is love and those who live in Him cannot do anything else than bring forth the fruits of love.

6. THE NEED OF OUR DAY—AND THROUGH IT GOD IS SPEAKING TO US—IMPERATIVELY DEMANDS THE UTMOST EFFORT TO HEAL THE DISMEMBERMENT OF THE CHRISTIAN CHURCH, TO MAKE CHRIST'S KINGDOM OF PEACE EFFECTUAL THROUGHOUT THE WORLD.

7. Freedom is not a matter of space but of spirit.

8. The Apostle Paul speaks of being steadfast in the faith. That is certainly the special grace for which we all must pray, we who live in a world opposed to faith. I had never before understood as I do here how solitary are believing Christians in the world. (In prison, 1943.)

9. I am glad and carefree [in prison, 1943] since I have put myself and my fate entirely into God's hands. Why should I fear? I am never bored here, as I have so much work to occupy me; the day hardly seems long enough. My chief anxiety is for the future of our nation. I am ready to suffer for that, yet I hope I may be allowed to work for it also.

10. IT IS THE VERY EXPERIENCE OF THIS WRETCHED WAR THAT IT AROUSES IN COUNTLESS PEOPLE THE LONGING FOR A GREAT EFFORT TO SAVE THE HUMAN RACE, AN EFFORT TO OVERCOME THE APPARENT POWERLESSNESS OF CHRISTIANITY IN ITS INFLUENCE ON WORLD EVENTS. ONLY WHEN WAR HAS THROWN THE NATIONS INTO UNSPEAKABLE MISERY WILL THE WHOLE WORLD BEGIN TO LOOK FOR A GREAT WORD OF REDEMPTION. BUT WHAT IS NEEDED CAN BE ATTEMPTED ONLY BY FAITH. GLOOMY AND HALFHEARTED EFFORTS ARE BOUND TO FAIL.

11. The unity of Christendom was the last will and Testament of Jesus Christ. The disunion of Christendom today contradicts the purpose of Our Lord and is a stumbling block to the world. To overcome these divisions is the task of every disciple of Christ.

12. Anyone who is familiar with the inner development of the churches separated from us will admit the truth of the following statement, that dogmatic differences—however serious and important—are not today the main element which hinders reunion. Much more important is the spiritual attitude on both sides.

13. The president of the German Freethinkers' Union until a day or two ago occupied the bed next to mine. In spite of the gulf which in the eyes of the world divided us, we were nearer to one another than were others because of our mutual respect. I could see that he was a man of noble character, and one who was a good friend. I could imagine that in him there survived subconsciously something of the Christian education which had come down through centuries of German history. I would count such a man as among Christ's company more than many baptized persons whose soul has remained untouched by the Spirit of Christ.

14. A feeling of disdain came over me when I heard the death sentence. I knew there was no shame, only honor, in being declared dishonorable by such a court.

15. ONLY A GREAT VENTURE OF FAITH, HUMILITY AND LOVE CAN SOLVE THE PROBLEM OF THE FATE OF CHRISTENDOM.

The Answer of Minerva

Pacifism and Resistance in Simone Weil

Like Bernanos and Camus, Simone Weil is one of those brilliant and independent French thinkers who were able to articulate the deepest concerns of France and Europe in the first half of this century. More controversial and perhaps more of a genius than the others, harder to situate, she has been called all kinds of names, both good and bad and often contradictory: Gnostic and Catholic, Jew and Albigensian, medievalist and modernist, Platonist and anarchist, rebel and saint, rationalist and mystic. De Gaulle said he thought she was out of her mind. The doctor in the sanatorium at Ashford, Kent, where she died (August 24, 1943) said, "She had a curious religious outlook and (probably) no religion at all." In any case, whatever is said about her, she can always be treated as "an enigma." Which is simply to say that she is somewhat more difficult to categorize than most people, since in her passion for integrity she absolutely refused to take up any position she had not first thought out in the light of what she believed to be a personal vocation to "absolute intellectual honesty." When she began to examine any accepted position, she easily detected its weaknesses and inconsistencies.

None of the books of Simone Weil (seventeen in French, eight in English) were written as books. They are all collections of notes, essays, articles, journals and letters. Though she has conquered a certain number of fans by the force of her personality, most readers remember her as the author of some fragment or other that they have found in some way both impressive and disconcerting. One cannot help admiring her lucid genius, and yet one can very easily disagree with her most fundamental and characteristic ideas. But this is usually because one does not see her thought as a whole. The new biography by Jacques Cabaud [1] not only tells of her active and tormented life,

1. Jacques Cabaud, *Simone Weil* (Harvill Press, 1964, 392 pp, ill.).

but studies in detail a large number of writings (of which a complete bibliography is given), together with the testimony of those who knew her. Cabaud has also avoided treating Simone Weil either as a problem or as a saint. He accepts her as she evidently was. Such a book is obviously indispensable, for without such a comprehensive and detached study it would be impossible to judge her reasonably. In fact, no one who reads this book carefully and dispassionately can treat Simone Weil merely as an enigma or a phenomenon, still less as deluded or irrelevant. Few writers have more significant thoughts on the history of our time and a better understanding of our calamities. On the other hand, probably not even Mr. Cabaud would claim that this book says the last word on Simone Weil or that it fully explains, for instance, her "Christian mysticism" that prompted her of deliberate purpose to remain outside the Church and refuse baptism even on the point of death because she felt that her natural element was with "the immense and unfortunate multitude of unbelievers." This "unbeliever," we note, was one who had been "seized" by Christ in a mystical experience the marks of which are to all appearances quite authentic, though the Catholic theologian has trouble keeping them clearly in a familiar and traditional focus. (Obviously, one of her charisms was that of living and dying as a sign of contradiction for Catholics, and one feels that the climate of Catholic thought in France at the time of Vatican II has been to some extent affected by at least a vague awareness of her experiences at Solesmes and Marseilles.)

Though her spirit was at times explicitly intended to be that of the medieval Cathars and though her description of her mystical life is strongly Gnostic and intellectual, she has had things to say of her experience of suffering and of her understanding of the suffering of Christ which are not only deeply Christian but also speak directly to the anguish and perplexity of modern man. This intuition of the nature and meaning of suffering provides, in Simone Weil, the core of a metaphysic, not to say a theology, of nonviolence. A metaphysic of nonviolence is something that the peace movement needs.

Looking back at Simone Weil's participation in the peace movement of the thirties, Cabaud speaks rather sweepingly of a collapse of pacifism in her thought and political action. It is quite true that the pacifism of the thirties was as naïve as it was popular, and that for many people at that time pacifism amounted to nothing more than the disposition to ignore unpleasant realities and to compromise with the threat of force as did Chamberlain at Munich. It is also true that Simone Weil herself underestimated the ruthlessness of Hitler at the time of the Munich crisis though her principles did not allow her to agree with the Munich pact. Cabaud quotes a statement of Simone Weil accusing herself of a "criminal error committed before 1939 with regard to pacifist groups and their actions." Her tolerance of a passive and inert pacifism was regarded by her as a kind of cooperation with "their disposition towards treason" which, she said, she did not see because she was disabled by illness (Cabaud, p. 197). This reflects her disgust with Vichy and with former pacifists who now submitted to Hitler without protest. But we cannot interpret this statement to mean that after Munich and then the fall of France Simone Weil abandoned all her former principles in order to take up an essentially new position in regard to war and peace. This would mean equating her "pacifism" with the quietism of the uncomprehending and the inert. It would also mean failure to understand that she became deeply committed to nonviolent resistance. Before Munich the emphasis was, however, on nonviolence, and after the fall of France the emphasis was on *resistance,* including the acceptance of resistance by force where nonviolence was ineffective.

It is unfortunate that Cabaud's book does not sufficiently avoid the usual cliché identification of pacifism as such with quietist passivity, and nonresistance. Simone Weil's love of peace was never sentimental and never quietistic; and though her judgment sometimes erred in assessing concrete situations, it was seldom unrealistic. An important article she wrote in 1937 remains one of the classic treatments of the problem of war and peace in our time. Its original title was: "Let us not start the Trojan War all over again." It appears in her *Selected Essays* as "The Power of Words." Cabaud analyzes it in his book (pp. 155–160) where he says that it marks a dividing line in her life. It belongs, in fact, to the same crucial period as her first mystical experiences.

There is nothing mystical about this essay. It develops a theme familiar to Montaigne and Charron—the most terrible thing about war is that, if it is examined closely, it is discovered to have no rationally definable objective. The supposed objectives of war are actually myths and fictions which are all the more capable of enlisting the full force of devotion to duty and hatred of the enemy when they are completely empty of content. Let us briefly resume this article, since it contains the substance of Simone Weil's ideas on peace and is (apart from some of her topical examples) just as relevant to our own time as it was to the late thirties.

The article begins with a statement which is passed over by Cabaud, and which is very important for us. Simone Weil remarks that while our technology has given us weapons of immense destructive power, the weapons do not go off by themselves (we hope). Hence it is a primordial mistake to think and act as if the weapons were what constituted our danger, rather than the people who are disposed to fire them off. But more precisely still: the danger lies not so much in this or that group or class but in the climate of thought in which all participate (not excluding pacifists). This is what Simone Weil set herself to understand. The theme of the article is, then, that war must be regarded as a problem to be solved by rational analysis and action, not as a fatality to which we must submit with bravery or desperation. We see immediately that she is anything but passively resigned to the evil of war. The acceptance of war as an unavoidable fatality she clearly saw to be the root of the power politician's ruthless and obsessed commitment to violence.

This, she believed, was the "key to our history."

If in fact conflicting statesmen faced one another only with clearly defined objectives that were fully rational, there would be a certain measure and limit which would permit of discussion and negotiation. But where the objectives are actually nothing more than capital-letter slogans without any intelligible content whatever, there is no common measure, therefore no possibility of communication, and hence no possibility of avoiding war except by ambiguous compromises, or by agreements that are not intended to be kept. Such agreements do not really avoid war. And of course they solve no problems.

The typology of the Trojan war, "known to every educated man," illustrates this. The only one, Greek or Trojan, who had any interest in Helen, was Paris. No one, Greek or Trojan, was fighting for Helen, but for the "real issue" which Helen symbolized. Unfortunately, there was no real issue at all for her to symbolize. Both armies, in this war, which is the type of all wars, were fighting in a moral void, motivated by symbols without content, which in the case of the Homeric heroes took the form of gods and myths. Simone Weil considered that this was relatively fortunate for them since their myths were thus kept within a well-defined area. For us, on the other hand (since we imagine that we have no myths at all), myth actually is without limitation and can easily penetrate the whole realm of political, social and ethical thought. Thus, instead of going to war because the gods have been arguing among themselves, we go because of "secret plots" and sinister combinations, because of political slogans elevated to the dignity of metaphysical absolutes: "Our political universe is peopled with myths and monsters—we know nothing there but absolutes." We shed blood for high-sounding words spelled out in capital letters. We seek to impart content to them by destroying other men who believe in enemy-words, also in capital letters.

But how can men really be brought to kill each other for what is objectively void? The nothingness of national, class or racial myth must receive an apparent substance, not from intelligible content but from the *will to destroy and be destroyed*. (We may observe here that the substance of idolatry is the willingness to give reality to metaphysical nothingness by sacrificing to it. The more totally one destroys present realities and alienates oneself to an object which is really void, the more total is the idolatry, i.e., the commitment to the falsehood that the non-entity is an objective absolute. Note here that in this context the God of the mystics is not "an object" and cannot be described properly as "an entity" among other entities. Hence one of the marks of authentic mysticism is that God as experienced by the mystic can in no way be the object of an idolatrous cult.)

The will to kill and be killed grows out of sacrifices and acts of destruction already performed. As soon as the war has begun, the first dead are there to demand further sacrifice from their companions since they have demonstrated by their example that the objective of the war is such that no price is too high to pay for its attainment. This is the "sledgehammer argument," the argument of Minerva in Homer: "You must fight on, for if you now make peace with the enemy, you will offend the dead."

These are cogent intuitions, but so far they do not add anything beyond their own vivacity to the ideas that prevailed in the thirties. In effect, everyone who remembered the First World War was capable of meditating on the futility of war in 1938. Everyone was still able to take sarcastic advantage of slogans about "making the world safe for democracy." But merely to say that war was totally absurd and totally meaningless, in its very nature, was to run the risk of missing the real point. Mere words without content do not suffice, of themselves, to start a war. Behind the empty symbols and the objectiveless motivation of force, there is a real force, the grimmest of all the social realities of our time: collective power, which Simone Weil, in her more Catharist mood, regarded as the "Great Beast." ("How will the soul be saved," she asked her philosophy students in the Lycée, "after the Great Beast has acquired an opinion about everything?")

The void underlying the symbols and the myths of nationalism, of capitalism, Communism, Fascism, racism, totalism, is in fact filled entirely by the presence of the Beast. We might say, developing her image, that the void thus becomes an insatiable demand for power, which sucks all life and all being into itself. Power is thus generated by the plunge of real and human values into nothingness, allowing themselves to be destroyed in order that the collectivity may attain to a theoretical and hopeless ideal of perfect and unassailable supremacy: "What is called national security is a chimerical state of things in which one would keep for oneself alone the power to make war while all other countries would be unable to do so. . . . War is therefore made *in order to keep or to increase the means of making war.* All international politics revolve in this vicious circle." "But," she adds, "why must one be able to make war? This no one knows any more than the Trojans knew why they had to keep Helen."

Nevertheless, when Germany overran France she herself found a reason for joining the resistance: the affirmation of human liberty against the abuse of power. "All over the world there are human beings *serving as means to the power of others without having con- sented to it.*" This was a basic evil that had to be resisted. The revision of Simone Weil's opinion on pacifism and nonviolence after Munich does not therefore resolve itself, as Cabaud seems to indicate, with a practical repudiation of both. Munich led her to clarify the distinction between ineffective and effective nonviolence. The former is what Gandhi called the nonviolence of the weak, and it merely submits to evil without resistance. Effective nonviolence ("the nonviolence of the strong") is that which opposes evil with serious and positive resistance, in order to overcome it with good. Simone Weil would apparently have added that if this nonviolence had no hope of success, then evil could be resisted by force. But she hoped for a state of affairs in which human conflict could be resolved nonviolently rather than by force. However, her notion of nonviolent resistance was never fully developed. If she had survived (she would be fifty-six now) she might possibly have written some exciting things on the subject.

Once this is understood, then we can also understand Simone Weil's revulsion at the collapse of that superficial and popular pacifism of Munich, which, since it was passive and also without clear objective, was only another moment in the objectiveless dialectic of brute power. And we can also understand the passion with which she sought to join the French resistance. But she did not change her principles. She did not commit herself to violent action, but she did seek to expose herself to the greatest danger and sacrifice, nonviolently. Though her desire to form a "front line nursing corps" (regarded by De Gaulle as lunacy) were never fulfilled, she nevertheless worked—indeed overworked—until the time of her death, trying to clarify the principles on which a new France could be built. She never gave up the hope that one might "substitute more and more in the world effective nonviolence for violence."

Auschwitz: A Family Camp

On December 20, 1963, twenty-two former SS men who had played important parts in the "final solution of the Jewish question" at Auschwitz went on trial at Frankfort. The trial lasted twenty months. Scores of survivors of the camp, together with many other witnesses, testified to the massive torture and butchery accomplished twenty years before, in that curious place "far away, somewhere in Poland." The testimony does not make pleasant reading. It fills a book [1] in large format running to nearly 450 pages: and this is only a summary of the most important points. The defendants were convicted and sentenced to prison terms, which they have all appealed. The most curious thing about the trial is that the defendants confidently and consistently denied almost everything. Finally the judge remarked in astonishment that he had "yet to meet anyone who had done anything at Auschwitz"! There was, in other words, a marked contrast between the unanimity of the witnesses saying black and the unanimity of the defendants saying white. Still more curiously, these same defendants had previously admitted much more of the dark side of the picture themselves. But now this has been "forgotten." They have somehow changed their minds. Hannah Arendt, in an important introduction, interprets this to mean that the German public has tacitly come to terms with the grim past. It has now apparently accepted these men, and many others like them.

In spite of the general tone of outrage still noticeable on the level of the court and of the better newspapers, the defendants themselves remained contemptuous and at ease, certain of ultimate freedom and confident that they had the tacit approval of their peers. Keeping this in mind, we now turn to the book. We reflect on the workings of a death factory where some three or four million people were barbarously

---

1. *Auschwitz*, by Bernd Naumann, translated by Jean Steinberg, with an introduction by Hannah Arendt (London: Pall Mall Press, 1966), 433 pp.

destroyed. Yet to judge by the testimony of these men who have been
sentenced to prison for literally thousands of murders each, the camp
was an innocent establishment, a place for "protective custody." It
doubtless knew its moments of austerity, but on the whole, it was
simply a camp where people went to be "reeducated." At times, it almost sounds like fairyland. . . .

Fairyland in Poland

Chief among the defendants was Robert Mulka. In July, 1942, Mulka
became deputy of the camp commandant, Hoss. Though second in
command for about a year, he claimed to know nothing about the fact
that many prisoners seemed to be dying and of course issued no orders
that had any connection with these unfortunate occurrences. When
questioned about his duties he said he had worried a lot about whether
or not the camp could afford some entertainers he wished to bring
there. He sometimes encountered death close at hand when he paraded
at the honor funeral of one of the SS guards. Gas chambers? Yes, he
had heard something about them over the camp grapevine. "Word,"
he said, "got out in the course of time." Crematory furnaces? He admitted having seen a red glow in the sky and wondered what it was:
rumor had supplied details. When pressed to explain why he had not
tried to discover the facts himself, he said there was "no one to ask."
Not even Commandant Hoss? No, the commandant was an "opaque
man." Were there no orders about the "special treatment" of "asocial
elements" and the "disinfection" of undesirables? He admitted that
"there were probably some general instructions" which of course
bypassed his own department, for he was after all only second in command. Confronted with orders signed by himself he offered no explanation. At the end of the trial, when the prosecution was asking that
Mulka be given life imprisonment for more than 36,500 murders,
Mulka himself simply asked the court to consider "all the circumstances
which at the time brought me into my conflict situation."

The other defendants all said the same. Even those who were accused of selecting the prisoners for extermination, of driving them into
the gas chambers, naked, with dogs turned loose and tearing their
flesh. Of beating them to death on the "Boger swing" in "rigorous
interrogations." Of injecting phenol into their hearts and killing them.
Of wiping them out in shootings that lasted two or three hours. All
these people were strangely unaware that Auschwitz had been an extermination camp and that they had been the exterminators. They admitted there were gas chambers "somewhere near the barracks." (And
where were the barracks? "Somewhere near the gas chambers!") Yes,
sometimes one drove a truck up "near the barracks" and one became
aware that "people were busy doing something." It was even observed

that "some prisoners were lying around." Resting perhaps? Since resting was not the usual thing at Auschwitz, were they perhaps dead? Altogether hard to say. One had failed to notice.

What about "cap shooting," making the prisoners throw their caps away, ordering them to run over to pick up the caps, and then shooting them for "trying to escape"? What about genuine escape attempts (some of which even succeeded)? One of the former SS guards assured the court that there were no attempted escapes. Who would want to escape? Auschwitz, he said, was after all, "a family camp." Another of the defendants, when obligingly describing the camp layout, asked the court if it would like him to point out on the map the place where he had made "a children's playground with sandboxes for the little ones."

Yes, there were even little ones in Auschwitz. They were marked out for play.

"The children were playing ball," says a former prisoner, "and waiting unsuspectingly. . . . A woman guard came, and clapped her hands, and called out: 'All right now, let's stop. Now we take showers.' And then they ran down the steps into the room in which they undressed. And the guard took a little girl on her arm and carried her down. And the child pointed to the eagle emblem on the cap of the SS woman and asked: 'What kind of birdie is that?' And that was the last I saw and heard of the child."

The Installations

No need to describe Auschwitz, the two huge death camps about three miles apart, the guard towers, the high barbwire fences charged with thousands of volts, the barracks, the gas chambers, the furnaces burning day and night. The evil-smelling smoke. The glare in the night sky visible for miles. The ramp where the long freight trains arrived, the "transports" jammed with prisoners, men, women, children, from all parts of Europe. On the ramp, those selected for immediate gassing were told by a gesture to go to the right. Selection depended to some extent on the caprice or mood of the one in charge. But one could be "selected" in the camp itself. If a prisoner became seriously ill or too weak to work. If the barracks were getting too crowded. If conditions became inconvenient, efficiency might demand a housecleaning.

Delousings were not working properly in the woman's camp. And a new doctor came along and solved the problem in a businesslike manner. "He simply had an entire block gassed." Having thus disposed of seven hundred and fifty women prisoners, he cleaned out the block, disinfected it, thoroughly deloused another batch of prisoners and moved them in. "He was the first to rid the entire women's camp of lice."

If Auschwitz was one of the main centers for the "final solution of the Jewish question" we must also remember it dealt with other problems too. Polish intellectuals and members of the Polish resistance were sent here for torture and liquidation. Thousands of Russian prisoners of war were exterminated at Auschwitz. According to the written testimony of one of the defendants (a deposition handed to the British at the end of the war) twelve thousand Russian prisoners of war reached Auschwitz early in 1942. In six months, there were only one hundred and fifty of them still alive. "Thousands of prisoners of war were shot in a copse near Birkenau" (wrote the defendant Perry Broad). They were "buried in mass graves . . . the fisheries began to complain that the fish in the ponds in the vicinity of Birkenau were dying. Experts said this was due to the pollution of the ground water through cadaveric poison. . . . The summer sun was beating down on Birkenau, the bodies . . . started to swell up and a dark red mass started to seep through the cracks of the earth. . . ." This called for a quick and efficient solution, since the camp authorities did not like bad publicity. Twenty or thirty "very reliable SS men" were picked for the job. They had to sign a statement that if they violated their oath of secrecy or even hinted at the nature of their job they would be punished by death. This special detail then rounded up prisoners to do the digging. The prisoners chosen were Jews. The bodies of the Russians were exhumed and burned. "For weeks, thick white smoke continued to rise from that isolated tract of land." There were rumors. Prisoners who refused to do this job were shot. The others did not survive to tell about it. The SS men on this unpleasant detail were rewarded with "special rations from the SS kitchen: 1 quart of milk, sausages, cigarettes and of course liquor." This, it turned out, was standard practice and applied also to those who had the tiresome job of beating prisoners to death, or shooting them at the Black Wall, or pushing them into the gas. When things were very busy the SS men were seen to be pretty drunk. On one such occasion an SS man, trying to show off his marksmanship, unfortunately shot a colleague. He was, of course, punished. One of the SS men, Klehr, was a male nurse— a "medical orderly." He specialized in injecting his patients in the heart with phenol and thus solving all their problems at once. He was also a notorious drunk, and was sometimes so intoxicated that he could no longer carry on the selections of appropriate candidates for the gas chamber. "Such selections had to be interrupted."

Klehr also had other hobbies. He was in charge of some rabbits: perhaps they were used for scientific experiments like the prisoners. At any rate he was so interested in the rabbits that he often "injected the prisoners two at a time because he wanted to get back to his rabbits." Such was the testimony of a former prisoner who had to hold the patients whom Klehr was injecting. One day the prisoner looked up and recognized the next patient in line. It was his father. Klehr was in a hurry and did not stop to ask why the prisoner was crying. He did so the next day, however. "Why," said Klehr in a burst of arbitrary generosity, "you should have told me. I would have let him live!"

Favors were sometimes done at Auschwitz! The prisoner, however, had feared to speak, convinced that if he did so he would have got a shot of phenol in the heart himself.

The Children of Zamosc

Klehr took care of one hundred and twenty Polish children from a village called Zamosc. They were killed in two batches: eighty the first day, the rest on the day after. Their parents were dead and no one quite knew what to do with them. They played in the courtyard of the hospital. "A ball had somehow turned up." Maybe that was when there were sandboxes. Another witness mentioned a balloon. But eventually the children were lined up and filed into the "examination room." Klehr was waiting for them with the syringe and the saucer of phenolic acid. The first ones screamed. After that it was somehow quieter. In the silence of the barrack, one heard the bodies falling off the chair and thumping onto the wooden floor. But Klehr did not do it all. Maybe he got bored and went to his rabbits, handing over the syringe. Scherpe, who took over, broke down under the strain and ran out of the room, refusing to kill any more children. A third SS man had to supply and finish the work begun. Reason for the death of the little boys from Zamosc? As a precaution against "immorality" in the camp. Auschwitz had to be very, very clean!

Other scenes with children: Outside the gas chambers and crematories where mothers with children were sent immediately upon arrival. The mothers sometimes tried to hide the children under the piles of clothing. "Sometimes the voice of a little child who had been forgotten would emerge from beneath a pile of clothing. . . . They would put a bullet through its head."

Sometimes, children were not sent at once for "special treatment." They might be kept handy for medical experiments. In the interests of science! Or they might even be assigned to useful work. One witness who entered Auschwitz at fourteen and survived testified that he was on the cart detail that removed ashes from the crematory. "We got ashes from Crematory III and scattered them on the icy roads. When there were no people in the gas chambers, the capo let us warm ourselves there." Another less bucolic scene: an SS man who threw living children into the flames and boiling human fat of the open cremation pyres. And finally this, from a witness: "Early in the morning I saw a little girl standing all by herself in the yard . . . wearing a claret-colored dress and [she had] a little pigtail. She held her hands at her side like a soldier. Once she looked down, wiped the dust off her shoes and again stood very still. Then I saw Boger come into the yard. He took the child by her hand—she went along very obediently—and stood her with her face to the Black Wall. Once she turned around. Boger again turned her head to the wall, walked back, and shot. . . ."

Exceptionally gentle for Boger, one of the most brutal professional butchers in the camp. He was sometimes seen to pick up little children by the heels and smash their heads against a brick wall. . . . But that was during a moment of stress in the mass liquidation of the Gypsy compound.

The Language of Auschwitz

Language itself has fallen victim to total war, genocide and systematic tyranny in our time. In destroying human beings, and human values, on a mass scale, the Gestapo also subjected the German language to violence and crude perversion.

In Auschwitz secrecy was emphasized. "If you talk about what you can see from here," one prisoner was told, "you'll go through the chimney." Written records were kept cryptic, evasive. Great care was taken to destroy as much paperwork as possible before the Russians arrived. Even mention of corporal punishment was taboo. Any open reference to the realities of life and death in the camp was regarded as treason. Any guard, doctor, prison administrator who let out the truth could be severely punished for "defeatist talk."

This circumlocution was itself highly significant. It admitted the sinister and ironic fact that even knowledge of the truth about Auschwitz could furnish a formidable propaganda weapon to the enemies of the Reich. The very irony of the fact should have raised some urgent questions about the principle behind the camp. But the function of doubletalk and doublethink is to say everything without raising inconvenient questions. Officialese has a talent for discussing reality while denying it and calling truth itself into question. Yet the truth remains. This doubletalk is by its very nature invested with a curious metaphysical leer. The language of Auschwitz is one of the vulnerable spots through which we get a clear view of the demonic.

Gestapo doubletalk encircles reality as a doughnut encircles its hole. "Special treatment," "special housing." We need no more than one lesson, and we gain the intuition which identifies the hole, the void of death, in the heart of the expression. When the circumlocution becomes a little more insistent ("recovery camps for the tired") it brings with it suggestions of awful lassitude, infinite hopelessness, as if meaning had now been abolished forever and we were definitively at the mercy of the absurd.

"Disinfectants," "materials for resettlement of Jews," "ovaltine substitute from Swiss Red Cross"—all references to Zyklon B! When a deadly poison gas is referred to as a soothing, restorative, a quasi-medicine to put babies to sleep, one senses behind the phrase a deep hatred of life itself. The key to Auschwitz language is its pathological joy in death. This turns out to be the key to all officialese. All of it is the celebration of boredom, of routine, of deadness, of organized futility. Auschwitz just carried the whole thing to its logical extreme, with a kind of heavy lilt in its mockery, its oafish love of death.

"Work makes free"—the sign over the gate of Auschwitz—tells, with grim satisfaction, the awful literal truth: "Here we work people to death." And behind it the dreadful metaphysical admission: "For us there is only one freedom, death."

"To the Bath," said the sign pointing to the gas chambers. (You will be purified of that dirty thing, your life!) And as a matter of fact the gas chambers and crematories were kept spotlessly clean. "Nothing was left of them [the victims] not even a speck of dust on the armatures."

"Assigned to harvest duty"—this, in the record of an SS man, meant he had been posted to Auschwitz. The double meaning of "harvest" was doubtless not random. It has an apocalyptic ring.

Yet the Gestapo people had an acute sense of the importance of words. One of them became quite excited in court, over the distinction between "transferred" and "assigned."

Those who tortured escapees or resistors (and resistance could be expressed even by an expressionless face) praised the "Boger Swing" as their most effective language machine. The victim was hung from a horizontal pole, upside down, by wrists and ankles. He was whipped so vigorously that he often spun clean round on the pole. "You'll learn to talk, we have language for you," said the Gestapo men. "My talking machine will make you talk," said Boger, who was proud of his invention. In fact he has earned himself a place in history on account of it. Not an enviable place.

One of the results of the Frankfort trial is that it makes an end of the pure Auschwitz myth: the myth of demented monsters who were twice our size, with six eyes and four rows of teeth, not of the same world as ourselves. The demonic sickness of Auschwitz emanated from ordinary people, stimulated by an extraordinary regime. The trial brought out their variety, their ordinariness, their shades of character, and even their capacity of change. In strict justice to Klehr, it must be said that he was profoundly affected by a visit from his wife in 1944, "a good kind woman . . . her two children were decent and well brought up." She did not suspect that her husband was involved in murder, but she knew that everything was not well at the camp. A witness overheard her saying to him, "I heard that terrible things happen here. I hope you're not involved." Klehr replied that he "cured people." But after his wife's visit, he began to treat prisoners more decently and to react against the camp methods. He even volunteered for frontline duty, and when his request was refused, he denounced a brutal camp officer and had him transferred, thus improving conditions.

It is nevertheless eerie to read the testimony of a witness who had been a neighbor of the defendant Dr. Capesius in Bucharest, and met him on the ramp where he sent her sisters, brothers and father to the gas chamber. "I still knew Dr. Capesius from Bucharest. . . . We lived in the same building. He was a representative of Bayer. Sometimes I spoke to him and his wife. . . ." The witness had even had coffee with Capesius and his wife in a park. That was the last time she saw him until 1944, at Auschwitz. "I recognized him right away. . . . I was happy to see him. When I stood in front of him all he said was, 'How old are you?' and sent me to the right." However, it may be noted that in sending her to the right he had saved her life. Not even Boger can be regarded without qualification as a pure monster. Auschwitz becomes a little more horrible when we have to admit that Boger too is a human being.

Boger and his colleagues were all more or less the products of a society at least as respectable and as civilized as that of New York or London. They had all received an education, some of them higher education. They had been brought up, it is said, in "Christian homes," or at least in middle-class homes—not quite the same, but Christianity has been willing to overlook the possible difference. Before Hitler, they lived and moved among "respectable people" and since Hitler they have done the same. How is it that for twelve years in between they could beat and bash and torment and shoot and whip and murder thousands of their fellow human beings, *including even their former neighbors and friends,* and think nothing of it?

In the first place it would be wrong to say that they all thought nothing of it. One among the defendants who comes close to being tragic is Dr. Lucas. We sense in him a complex, lonely, tormented character who knew he was involved in a wrong that he could not entirely escape. Perhaps he might have escaped it. No one will ever be able to say with finality. But in any event he elected to go along with the system, to participate in the "selections," while at the same time practicing the ambivalent quasi-unconscious resistance technique of the "good soldier Schweik." Witness after witness spoke out in favor of Dr. Lucas. He was different from the others. Yes, he sent people to their death, but many witnesses recognized that he had saved their lives. Still he remained identified with the machinery of organized murder, and recognized that in so doing he had ruined his own life. Another who admitted that Auschwitz had been a doubtful quality in his life was Stark. He had gone to the camp as an SS guard when still in his teens. He had not yet finished school. Shooting, beating and killing were, for him, normal facts of life. He accepted them without question. He had practically grown up under Hitler and did not learn the difference until later. "I regret the mistakes of my past," he said, "but I cannot undo them."

What about Boger? Though he consistently denied everything said by witnesses, in the end his defense was content to ask for leniency rather than life imprisonment, on the grounds that Boger had merely done his duty as a good policeman.

This seems to sum up Boger's rather aggrieved view of his own case. Boger defended his "swing" right to the end. How could one refuse a conscientious police official the right to use "rigorous methods of interrogation"? Boger bluntly addressed the court on the virtues and necessity of these methods. They were highly practical. His defense lawyer expostulated with the Jury: "The swing was not intended as torture: it was the only effective means of physical suasion."

The shocking thing about the views of both Boger and his lawyer is that they are evidently quite sincere. Not only that, they are views with which, it is assumed, other people will sympathize without difficulty.

In his final statement to the court, Boger made a distinction between the genocidal extermination of the Jews, which he admitted was perhaps a bit rough, and what he himself thought most important at the time: "*the fight against the Polish resistance movement and Bolshevism.*"

Boger's case has now become an open appeal to the "good Germans" who, he assumes, agree with him; they will easily approve the rigors of his interrogation methods since they were justified by anti-Communism.

At this point, there swims into view a picture taken at another investigation, (hardly a trial) in the state of Mississippi. We see the smiling, contemptuous, brutal faces of the police deputies and their colleagues who are allegedly the murderers of three civil rights workers in the summer of 1964. Whatever may have been the facts in the case, one feels that in Mississippi and Auschwitz the basic assumptions are not very different. Instead of seeing the Bogers and Klehrs of Auschwitz as fabulous, myth-sized and inhuman monsters, we come to recognize that people like them are in fact all around us. All they need is the right kind of crisis, and they will blossom out.

Salutary Reflections

Such is the first conclusion. We have learned to associate the incredible brutality and inhumanity of Auschwitz with ordinary respectable people, in an extraordinary situation.

Second: Auschwitz worked because these people wanted it to work. Instead of resisting it, rebelling against it, they put the best of their energies into making genocide a success. This was true not only of one or two psychopaths but of an entire bureaucratic officialdom, including not only the secret police and Nazi party members but also managers and employees of the industries which knowingly made use of the slave labor provided in such abundance by the camp.

Third: although it was usual to argue that "they had no choice" and that they were "forced" to comply with orders, the trial showed a more complex and less excusable picture of the defendants. Almost all of them committed gratuitous acts of arbitrary cruelty and violence which were forbidden even by the Gestapo's own rules. Some were even punished by the SS for these violations. Was there no choice? There are on record refusals of men who simply would not take part in murder and got themselves transferred. Why was not this done more often? Let us clearly spell out two of the circumstances. Auschwitz was safe. One was not at the front, and there was practically no danger from bombing planes. And there were privileges: the work was no doubt disagreeable to some, but there were extra rations, smokes, drinks. Finally, there can be little doubt that many of these men tortured and killed because they thoroughly enjoyed it.

Fourth: what does all this add up to? Given the right situation and another Hitler, places like Auschwitz can be set up, put into action, kept running smoothly, with thousands of people systematically starved, beaten, gassed, and whole crematories going full blast. Such camps can be set up tomorrow anywhere and made to work with the greatest efficiency, because there is no dearth of people who would be glad to do the job, provided it is sanctioned by authority. They will be glad because they will instinctively welcome and submit to an ideology which enables them to be violent and destructive without guilt. They are happy with a belief which turns them loose against their fellow man to destroy him cruelly and without compunction, as long as he belongs to a different race, or believes in a different set of semi-meaningless political slogans.

It is enough to affirm one basic principle: ANYONE BELONGING TO CLASS X OR NATION Y OR RACE Z IS TO BE REGARDED AS SUBHUMAN AND WORTHLESS, AND CONSEQUENTLY HAS NO RIGHT TO EXIST. All the rest will follow without difficulty.

As long as this principle is easily available, as long as it is taken for granted, as long as it can be spread out on the front pages at a moment's notice and accepted by all, we have no need of monsters: ordinary policemen and good citizens will take care of everything.

A Devout Meditation
in Memory of Adolf Eichmann

One of the most disturbing facts that came out in the Eichmann trial
was that a psychiatrist examined him and pronounced him *perfectly
sane*. I do not doubt it at all, and that is precisely why I find it
disturbing.

If all the Nazis had been psychotics, as some of their leaders probably were, their appalling cruelty would have been in some sense
easier to understand. It is much worse to consider this calm, "well-
balanced," unperturbed official conscientiously going about his desk
work, his administrative job which happened to be the supervision of
mass murder. He was thoughtful, orderly, unimaginative. He had a
profound respect for system, for law and order. He was obedient, loyal,
a faithful officer of a great state. He served his government very well.

He was not bothered much by guilt. I have not heard that he developed any psychosomatic illnesses. Apparently he slept well. He had
a good appetite, or so it seems. True, when he visited Auschwitz, the
Camp Commandant, Hoss, in a spirit of sly deviltry, tried to tease the
big boss and scare him with some of the sights. Eichmann was disturbed, yes. He was disturbed. Even Himmler had been disturbed, and
had gone weak at the knees. Perhaps, in the same way, the general
manager of a big steel mill might be disturbed if an accident took
place while he happened to be somewhere in the plant. But of course
what happened at Auschwitz was not an accident: just the routine
unpleasantness of the daily task. One must shoulder the burden of
daily monotonous work for the Fatherland. Yes, one must suffer dis-
comfort and even nausea from unpleasant sights and sounds. It all
comes under the heading of duty, self-sacrifice, and obedience. Eichmann was devoted to duty, and proud of his job.

The sanity of Eichmann is disturbing. We equate sanity with a sense
of justice, with humaneness, with prudence, with the capacity to love
and understand other people. We rely on the sane people of the world

to preserve it from barbarism, madness, destruction. And now it begins to dawn on us that it is precisely the *sane* ones who are the most dangerous.

It is the sane ones, the well-adapted ones, who can without qualms and without nausea aim the missiles and press the buttons that will initiate the great festival of destruction that they, *the sane ones,* have prepared. What makes us so sure, after all, that the danger comes from a psychotic getting into a position to fire the first shot in a nuclear war? Psychotics will be suspect. The sane ones will keep them far from the button. No one suspects the sane, and the sane ones will have *perfectly good reasons,* logical, well-adjusted reasons, for firing the shot. They will be obeying sane orders that have come sanely down the chain of command. And because of their sanity they will have no qualms at all. When the missiles take off, then, *it will be no mistake.*

We can no longer assume that because a man is "sane" he is therefore in his "right mind." The whole concept of sanity in a society where spiritual values have lost their meaning is itself meaningless. A man can be "sane" in the limited sense that he is not impeded by his disordered emotions from acting in a cool, orderly manner, according to the needs and dictates of the social situation in which he finds himself. He can be perfectly "adjusted." God knows, perhaps such people can be perfectly adjusted even in hell itself.

And so I ask myself: what is the meaning of a concept of sanity that excludes love, considers it irrelevant, and destroys our capacity to love other human beings, to respond to their needs and their sufferings, to recognize them also as persons, to apprehend their pain as one's own? Evidently this is not necessary for "sanity" at all. It is a religious notion, a spiritual notion, a Christian notion. What business have we to equate "sanity" with "Christianity"? None at all, obviously. The worst error is to imagine that a Christian must try to be "sane" like everybody else, that we *belong* in our kind of *society.* That we must be "realistic" about it. We must develop a *sane* Christianity: and there have been plenty of sane Christians in the past. Torture is nothing new, is it? We ought to be able to rationalize a little brainwashing, and genocide, and find a place for nuclear war, or at least for napalm bombs, in our moral theology. Certainly some of us are doing our best along those lines already. There are hopes! Even Christians can shake off their sentimental prejudices about charity, and become sane like Eichmann. They can even cling to a certain set of Christian formulas, and fit them into a Totalist Ideology. Let them talk about justice, charity, love, and the rest. These words have not stopped some sane men from acting very sanely and cleverly in the past. . . .

No, Eichmann was sane. The generals and fighters on both sides, in World War II, the ones who carried out the total destruction of entire cities, these were the sane ones. Those who have invented and developed atomic bombs, thermonuclear bombs, missiles; who have planned the strategy of the next war; who have evaluated the various possibilities of using bacterial and chemical agents: these are not the crazy people, they are the *sane* people. The ones who coolly estimate how many millions of victims can be considered expendable in a nuclear war, I presume they do all right with the Rorschach ink blots too. On the other hand, you will probably find that the pacifists and the ban-the-bomb people are, quite seriously, just as we read in *Time*, a little crazy.

I am beginning to realize that "sanity" is no longer a value or an end in itself. The "sanity" of modern man is about as useful to him as the huge bulk and muscles of the dinosaur. If he were a little less sane, a little more doubtful, a little more aware of his absurdities and contradictions, perhaps there might be a possibility of his survival. But if he is sane, too sane . . . perhaps we must say that in a society like ours the worst insanity is to be totally without anxiety, totally "sane."

II

THE
NONVIOLENT
ALTERNATIVE

Faith and Violence

By Way of Preface

The Hassidic rabbi Ball-shem-tov once told the following story. Two men were traveling through a forest. One was drunk, the other was sober. As they went, they were beset by robbers, beaten, robbed of all they had, even their clothing. When they emerged, people asked them if they got through the wood without trouble. The drunken man said: "Everything was fine: nothing went wrong: we had no trouble at all!"

They said: "How does it happen that you are naked and covered with blood?"

He did not have an answer.

The sober man said: "Do not believe him: he is drunk. It was a disaster. Robbers beat us without mercy and took everything we had. Be warned by what happened to us, and look out for yourselves."

For some "faithful"—and for unbelievers too—"faith" seems to be a kind of drunkenness, an anaesthetic, that keeps you from realizing and believing that anything can ever go wrong. Such faith can be immersed in a world of violence and make no objection: the violence is perfectly all right. It is quite normal—unless of course it happens to be exercised by Negroes. Then it must be put down instantly by superior force. The drunkenness of this kind of faith—whether in a religious message or merely in a political ideology—enables us to go through life without seeing that our own violence is a disaster and that the overwhelming force by which we seek to assert ourselves and our own self-interest may well be our ruin.

Is faith a narcotic dream in a world of heavily-armed robbers, or is it an awakening?

Is faith a convenient nightmare in which we are attacked and obliged to destroy our attackers?

What if we awaken to discover that *we* are the robbers, and our destruction comes from the root of hate in ourselves?

Abbey of Gethsemani
ADVENT, 1967

Part One: Toward a Theology of Resistance

Theology today needs to focus carefully upon the crucial problem of violence. The commandment "Thou shalt not kill" is more than a mere matter of academic or sentimental interest in an age when man not only is more frustrated, more crowded, more subject to psychotic and hostile delusion than ever, but also has at his disposition an arsenal of weapons that make global suicide an easy possibility. But the so-called nuclear umbrella has not simplified matters in the least: it may have (at least temporarily) caused the nuclear powers to reconsider their impulses to reduce one another to radioactive dust. But meanwhile "small" wars go on with unabated cruelty, and already more bombs have been exploded on Vietnam than were dropped in the whole of World War II. The population of the affluent world is nourished on a steady diet of brutal mythology and hallucination, kept at a constant pitch of high tension by a life that is intrinsically violent in that it forces a large part of the population to submit to an existence which is humanly intolerable. Hence murder, mugging, rape, crime, corruption. But it must be remembered that the crime that breaks out of the ghetto is only the fruit of a greater and more pervasive violence: the injustice which forces people to live in the ghetto in the first place. The problem of violence, then, is not the problem of a few rioters and rebels, but the problem of a whole social structure which is outwardly ordered and respectable, and inwardly ridden by psychopathic obsessions and delusions.

It is perfectly true that violence must at times be restrained by force: but a convenient mythology which simply legalizes the use of force by big criminals against little criminals—whose small-scale criminality is largely *caused* by the large-scale injustice under which they live—only perpetuates the disorder.

Pope John XXIII in *Pacem in Terris* quoted, with approval, a famous saying of Saint Augustine: "What are kingdoms without justice but large bands of robbers?" The problem of violence today must be traced to its root: not the small-time murderers but the massively organized bands of murderers whose operations are global.

This book is concerned with the defense of the dignity and rights of man against the encroachments and brutality of massive power structures which threaten either to enslave him or to destroy him, while exploiting him in their conflicts with one another.

The Catholic moral theology of war has, especially since the Renaissance, concerned itself chiefly with casuistical discussion of how far the monarch or the sovereign state can justly make use of force. The historic context of this discussion was the struggle for a European balance of power, waged for absolute monarchs by small professional armies. In a new context we find not only a new struggle on a global scale between mammoth nuclear powers provided with arsenals capable of wiping out the human race, but also the emergence of scores of small nations in an undeveloped world that was until recently colonial. In this Third World we find not huge armed establishments but petty dictatorships (representing a rich minority) opposed by small, volunteer guerrilla bands fighting for "the poor." The Great Powers tend to intervene in these struggles, not so much by the threat and use of nuclear weapons (with which, however, they continue to threaten one another) but with armies of draftees and with new experimental weapons which are sometimes incredibly savage and cruel and which are used mostly against helpless non-combatants. Although many churchmen, moved apparently by force of habit, continue to issue mechanical blessings upon these draftees and upon the versatile applications of science to the art of killing, it is evident that this use of force does not become moral just because the government and the mass media have declared the cause to be patriotic. The cliché "my country right or wrong" does not provide a satisfactory theological answer to the moral problems raised by the intervention of American power in all parts of the Third World. And in fact the Second Vatican Council, following the encyclical of John XXIII *Pacem in Terris,* has had some pertinent things to say about war in the nuclear era.

To assert that conflict resolution is one of the crucial areas of theological investigation in our time is not to issue an *a priori* demand for a theology of pure pacifism. To declare that *all* use of force in any way whatever is by the very fact immoral is to plunge into confusion and unreality from the very start, because, as John XXIII admitted, "unfortunately the law of fear still reigns among peoples" and there are situations in which the only way to effectively protect human life and rights is by forcible resistance against unjust encroachment. Murder is not to be passively permitted, but resisted and prevented—and all the more so when it becomes mass murder. The problem arises not when theology admits that force can be necessary, but when it does so in a way that implicitly favors the claims of the powerful and self-seeking establishment against the common good of mankind or against the rights of the oppressed.

The real moral issue of violence in the twentieth century is obscured by archaic and mythical presuppositions. We tend to judge violence in terms of the individual, the messy, the physically disturbing, the personally frightening. The violence we want to see restrained is the violence of the hood waiting for us in the subway or the elevator. That is reasonable, but it tends to influence us too much. It makes us think that the problem of violence is limited to this very small scale, and it makes us unable to appreciate the far greater problem of the more abstract, more global, more organized presence of violence on a massive and corporate pattern. Violence today is *white-collar violence, the systematically organized bureaucratic and technological destruction of man.*

The theology of violence must not lose sight of the real problem, which is not the individual with a revolver but *death and even genocide as big business.* But this big business of death is all the more innocent and effective because it involves a long chain of individuals, each of whom can feel himself absolved from responsibility, and each of whom can perhaps salve his conscience by contributing with a more *meticulous efficiency* to his part in the massive operation.

We know, for instance, that Adolph Eichmann and others like him felt no guilt for their share in the extermination of the Jews. This feeling of justification was due partly to their absolute obedience to higher authority and partly to the care and efficiency which went into the details of their work. This was done almost entirely on paper. Since they dealt with numbers, not with people, and since their job was one of abstract bureaucratic organization, apparently they could easily forget the reality of what they were doing. The same is true to an even greater extent in modern warfare in which the real moral problems are not to be located in rare instances of hand-to-hand combat, but in the remote planning and organization of technological destruction. The real crimes of modern war are committed not at the front (if any) but in war offices and ministries of defense in which no one ever has to see any blood unless his secretary gets a nosebleed. Modern technological mass murder is not directly visible, like individual murder. It is abstract, corporate, businesslike, cool, free of guilt feelings and therefore a thousand times more deadly and effective than the eruption of violence out of individual hate. It is this polite, massively organized white-collar murder machine that threatens the world with destruction, not the violence of a few desperate teen-agers in a slum. But our antiquated theology, myopically focused on *individual* violence alone, fails to see this. It shudders at the fantasm of muggings and killings where a mess is made on our own doorstep, but blesses and canonizes the antiseptic violence of corporately organized murder because it is respectable, clean, and above all profitable.

In another place I have contrasted, in some detail, the mentality of John XXIII on this point with the mentality of Machiavelli (see *Seeds of Destruction,* Part III). Machiavelli said: "There are two methods of fighting, one by law and the other by force. The first method is that of men, the second of beasts; but as the first method is often insufficient, one must have recourse to the second." I submit that a theology which merely seeks to justify the "method of beasts" and to help it disguise itself as law—since it is after all a kind of "prolongation of law"—is not adequate for the problems of a time of violence.

On the other hand we also have to recognize that when oppressive power is thoroughly well established, it does not always need to resort openly to the "method of beasts" because its laws are already powerful —perhaps also bestial—enough. In other words, when a system can, without resort to overt force, *compel* people to live in conditions of abjection, helplessness, wretchedness that keep them on the level of beasts rather than of men, it is plainly violent. To make men live on a subhuman level against their will, to constrain them in such a way that they have no hope of escaping their condition, is an unjust exercise of force. Those who in some way or other concur in the oppression—and perhaps profit by it—are exercising violence even though they may be preaching pacifism. And their supposedly peaceful laws, which maintain this spurious kind of order, are in fact instruments of violence and oppression. If the oppressed try to resist by force—which is their right—theology has no business preaching nonviolence to them. Mere blind destruction is, of course, futile and immoral: but who are we to condemn a desperation we have helped to cause!

However, as John XXIII pointed out, the "law of fear" is not the only law under which men can live, nor is it really the normal mark of the human condition. To live under the law of fear and to deal with one another by "the methods of beasts" will hardly help world events "to follow a course in keeping with man's destiny and dignity." In order for us to realize this, we must remember that "one of the profound requirements of [our] nature is this: . . . it is not fear that should reign but love—a love that tends to express itself in mutual collaboration."

"Love" is unfortunately a much misused word. It trips easily off the Christian tongue—so easily that one gets the impression it means others ought to love us for standing on their necks.

A theology of love cannot afford to be sentimental. It cannot afford to preach edifying generalities about charity, while identifying "peace" with mere established power and legalized violence against the oppressed. A theology of love cannot be allowed merely to serve the interests of the rich and powerful, justifying their wars, their violence and their bombs, while exhorting the poor and underprivileged to practice patience, meekness, long-suffering and to solve their problems, if at all, nonviolently.

The theology of love must seek to deal realistically with the evil and injustice in the world, and not merely to compromise with them. Such a theology will have to take note of the ambiguous realities of politics, without embracing the specious myth of a "realism" that merely justifies force in the service of established power. Theology does not exist merely to appease the already too untroubled conscience of the powerful and the established. A theology of love may also conceivably turn out to be a theology of revolution. In any case, it is a theology of *resistance,* a refusal of the evil that reduces a brother to homicidal desperation.

On the other hand, Christian faith and purity of intention—the simplicity of the dove—are no guarantee of political acumen, and theological insight is no substitute for the wisdom of the serpent which is seldom acquired in Sunday school. Should the theologian or the priest be too anxious to acquire that particiular kind of wisdom? Should he be too ambitious for the achievements of a successful political operator? Should he be more careful to separate authentic Christian witness from effectiveness in political maneuvering? Or is the real place of the priest the place which Fr. Camilo Torres took, with the Colombian guerrillas?

This book cannot hope to answer such questions. But it can at least provide a few materials for a theology, not of pacifism and nonviolence in the sense of *nonresistance,* but for a theology of resistance which is at the same time *Christian* resistance and which therefore emphasizes reason and humane communication rather than force, but which also admits the possibility of force in a limit situation when everything else fails.

Such a theology could not claim to be Christian if it did not retain at least some faith in the meaning of the Cross and of the redemptive death of Jesus who, instead of using force against his accusers, took all the evil upon himself and overcame that evil by his suffering. This is a basic Christian pattern, but a realistic theology will, I believe, give a new practical emphasis to it. Instead of preaching the Cross *for others* and advising them to suffer patiently the violence which we sweetly impose on them, with the aid of armies and police, we might conceivably recognize the right of the less fortunate to use force, and study more seriously the practice of nonviolence and humane methods on our own part when, as it happens, we possess the most stupendous arsenal of power the world has ever known.

General MacArthur was no doubt sincerely edified when the conquered Japanese wrote into their constitution a clause saying they would never again arm and go to war. He warmly congratulated them for their wisdom. But he never gave the slightest hint of thinking the United States ought to follow their example. On the contrary, he maintained to the end that for *us* there could be no other axiom than that "there is no substitute for victory." Others have come after him with even more forceful convictions. They would probably be glad to see all Asian nations disarm on the spot; but failing that, we can always bomb them back to the stone age. And there is no reason to believe that the United States may not eventually try to do so.

The title of this book is *Faith and Violence.* This might imply several interesting possibilities. The book might, for instance, study the violence of believers—and this, as history shows, has sometimes been considerable. The disciples of the King of Peace have sometimes managed to prove themselves extremely bloodthirsty, particularly among themselves. They have rather consistently held, in practice, that the way to prove the sincerity of faith was not so much nonviolence as the generous use of lethal weapons. It is a curious fact that in this present century there have been two world wars of unparalleled savagery in which Christians, on both sides, were exhorted to go out and kill each other if not in the name of Christ and faith, at least in the name of "Christian duty." One of the strange facts about this was that, in the Second World War, German Christians were exhorted by their pastors to die for a government that was not only non-Christian but anti-Christian and which had evident intentions of getting rid of the Church. An official theology which urged Christians, as a matter of Christian duty, to fight for such a government surely calls for examination. And we shall see that few questioned it. Few question it still. One man did, and we shall devote a few pages to his unusual case. Possibly he was what the Catholic Church might conceivably call a "saint." If so, it was because he dared to refuse military service under the Fuehrer whom his bishop told him he was obliged to obey.

In the case of Franz Jägerstätter we have a faith that stood up against an unjust but established power and refused to practice in the service of that power. On the other side, we have Simone Weil who was a French pacifist before World War II and who later joined the French resistance against the Nazis. Simone was not a Christian in the official sense of the word, but no matter; her motives and reservations were Christian, and the limits which she set to force when she decided to resist were also Christian.

Father Delp, Franz Jägerstätter and Simone Weil all resisted the same evil, the same violent, destructive and antihuman political force of Nazism, and they all resisted it for the same motives. Their resistance took somewhat different forms. But one can see in them three possible examples of Christian resistance. In each case the resistance was more or less nonviolent. It might conceivably have involved a use of force (as in the case of those Christians who plotted against Hitler's life—as Father Delp was accused of doing). The point to be emphasized, however, is not only that these Christians were nonviolent but that they *resisted*. They refused to submit to a force which they recognized as antihuman and utterly destructive. They refused to accept this evil and to palliate it under the guise of "legitimate authority." In doing so they proved themselves better theologians than the professionals and the pontiffs who supported that power and made others obey it, thus cooperating in the evil.

The first section of this book studies various aspects of nonviolent resistance to the evil of war as waged by the "large bands of robbers." Its approach assumes that nonviolent resistance can be an effective means of conflict resolution, perhaps more effective than the use of force. At no point in these pages will the reader find the author trying to prove that evil should not be resisted. The reason for emphasizing nonviolent resistance is this: he who resists force with force in order to seize power may become contaminated by the evil which he is resisting and, when he gains power, may be just as ruthless and unjust a tyrant as the one he has dethroned. A nonviolent victory, while far more difficult to achieve, stands a better chance of curing the illness instead of contracting it.

There is an essential difference here, for nonviolence seeks to "win" not by destroying or even by humiliating the adversary, but by *convincing him* that there is a higher and more certain common good than can be attained by bombs and blood. Nonviolence, ideally speaking, does not try to overcome the adversary by winning over him, but to turn him from an adversary into a collaborator by winning him over. Unfortunately, nonviolent resistance as practiced by those who do not understand it and have been trained in it is often only a weak and veiled form of psychological aggression.

The second part of the book, devoted to Vietnam, takes into account the fact that the use of force in Vietnam is curing and settling nothing. With incredible expense and complication, and with appalling consequences to the people we claim to be helping, we are inexorably destroying the country we want to "save." The Third Part considers the racial conflict in the United States, where nonviolence was first adopted as the best method and later discredited as ineffective, in favor of an appeal to force. The last section considers the rather ambiguous "death of God" which has curiously coincided with these other events and may perhaps cast some light on them.

At any rate, faith itself is in crisis along with the society which was once officially Christian, officially supported by God and his representatives, and which is now seeking to consolidate itself by an ever more insistent appeal to violence and brute power.

In brief: without attempting a systematic treatment of that theology of love which, in crisis situations, may become a theology of resistance, we will examine principles and cases all of which help us to see the unacceptable ambiguities of a theology of "might makes right" masquerading as a Christian theology of love.

Part Two: The Vietnam War: An Overwhelming Atrocity

No country may unjustly oppress others or unduly meddle in their affairs.

(*Pacem in Terris*, n.120)

As men in their private enterprises cannot pursue their own interests to the detriment of others, so too states cannot lawfully seek that development of their own resources which brings harm to other states and unjustly oppresses them.

(*Pacem in Terris*, n.92)

In 1967 several young members of the International Volunteer
Service in Vietnam resigned and returned to America, in protest
against the way the war was, in their opinion, needlessly and hopelessly ravaging the country.

The International Volunteer Service is a nonprofit organization
meant to help American youth to contribute to international goodwill
by person-to-person contracts and service programs in other countries.
Ambassador Lodge had called it "one of the success stories of American
assistance," and obviously the men serving in Vietnam were in very
close touch with the people, knew the language, and were perhaps
better able to judge the state of affairs than most other Americans.
As they said, they "dealt with people, not statistics," and they were in
a position to know that the story of the Vietnam war is a very different
one when it is learned from women and children whose flesh has
been burned by napalm than it is when those same women and
children appear in statistics as "enemy" casualities.

At this point, in case the reader is not fully aware of what napalm
is, we might quote from a report of four American physicians on
"Medical Problems of South Vietnam":

> Napalm is a highly sticky inflammable jelly which clings to
> anything it touches and burns with such heat that all oxygen
> in the area is exhausted within moments. Death is either by
> roasting or suffocation. Napalm wounds are often fatal (esti-
> mates are 90%). Those who survive face a living death. The
> victims are frequently children.

Another American physician wrote (Dr. R. E. Perry, *Redbook*, January,
1967):

> I have been an orthopedic surgeon for a good number of
> years with rather a wide range of medical experience. But
> nothing could have prepared me for my encounters with
> Vietnamese women and children burned by napalm. It was
> shocking and sickening even for a physician to see and smell
> the blackened and burned flesh.

By their resignation and by the statement they issued in an open
letter to President Johnson, these men attempted to get through to
the American public with a true idea of what the war really means
to the Vietnamese—our allies, the ones we are supposedly "saving"
from Communism. The attitude and feelings of the Vietnamese
people (as distinct from the government) are too little known in the
United States. They have been systematically ignored. Pictures of
GIs bestowing candy bars upon half-naked "native" children are
supposed to give us all the information we need in this regard. These
are happy people who love our boys because we are saving them

from the Reds and teaching them "democracy." It is of course important, psychologically and politically, for the public to believe this because otherwise the war itself would be questioned, and as a matter of fact it *is* questioned. Never was there a war in American history that was so much questioned! The official claim that such questioning is "betrayal" is a transparently gross and authoritarian attack on democratic liberty.

According to these Americans in the International Volunteer Service, men who cannot be considered leftists, still less as traitors, the American policy of victory at any price is simply destroying Vietnam. It is quite possible that the United States may eventually "win," but the price may be so high that there will be few left around to enjoy the fruits of victory and democracy in a country which we will, of course, obligingly reconstruct according to ideas of our own.

The people of South Vietnam have already had some experience of this kind of resettlement and reconstruction. Having seen their own homes burned or bulldozed out of existence, their fields and crops blasted with defoliants and herbicides, their livelihood and culture destroyed, they have been forcibly transplanted into places where they cannot live as they would like or as they know how, and forced into a society where, to adapt and be "at home" one has to be a hustler, a prostitute, or some kind of operator who knows how to get where the dollars are.

The people we are "liberating" in Vietnam are caught between two different kinds of terrorism, and the future presents them with nothing but a more and more bleak and hopeless prospect of unnatural and alienated existence. From their point of view, it doesn't matter much who wins. Either way it is going to be awful: but at least if the war can stop before everything is destroyed, and if they can somehow manage their own destiny, they will settle for that.

This, however, does not fit in with our ideas. We intend to go on bombing, burning, killing, bulldozing and moving people around while the numbers of plague victims begin to mount sharply and while the "civilization" we have brought becomes more and more rotten. The people of South Vietnam believe that we are supporting a government of wealthy parasites they do not and cannot trust. They believe that the 1967 election was rigged, and they know that the two newspapers which protested about it were immediately silenced and closed down by the "democratic" government which we are supporting at such cost.

To put it plainly, according to the men who resigned from the International Volunteer Service the people of South Vietnam are hardly grateful for "democracy" on such terms, and while they are quite willing to accept our dollars when they have a chance, they do not respect us or trust us. In point of fact, they have begun to hate us.

Far from weakening Communism in Asia by our war policy, we are only strengthening it. The Vietnamese are no lovers of China, but by the ruthlessness of our war for "total victory" we are driving them into the arms of the Red Chinese. "The war as it is now being waged," say the Volunteers, "is self-defeating." They support their contentions by quoting people they have known in Vietnam.

A youth leader: "When the Americans learn to respect the true aspirations in Vietnam, true nationalism will come to power. Only true nationalists can bring peace to the South, talk to the North and bring unification."

While a Catholic bishop in the United States was soothing President Johnson with the assurance the war in Vietnam is "a sad and heavy obligation imposed by the mandate of love," a Buddhist nun said in Vietnam: "You Americans come to help the Vietnamese people, but have brought only death and destruction. Most of us Vietnamese hate from the bottom of our hearts the Americans who have brought the suffering of this war. . . ." After which she burned herself to death. That, too, was a drastic act of violence. Whether or not we may agree with it, we must admit that it lends a certain air of seriousness to her denunciation! Unfortunately, such seriousness does not seem to get through to those Americans who most need to hear and understand it.

Meanwhile Billy Graham declared that the war in Vietnam was a "spiritual war between good and evil." A plausible statement, certainly, but not in the way in which he meant it. At the same time a Saigon Catholic Youth leader gave another view of the picture: "We are caught in a struggle between two power blocs. . . . Many people told me you cannot trust Americans, but I never accepted it. Now I am beginning to believe it. You come to help my people, but they will hate you for it."

The tragic thing about Vietnam is that, after all, the "realism" of our program there is so unrealistic, so rooted in myth, so completely out of touch with the needs of the people whom we know only as statistics and to whom we never manage to listen, except where they fit in with our psychopathic delusions. Our external violence in Vietnam is rooted in an inner violence which simply ignores the human reality of those we claim to be helping. The result of this at home has been an ever-mounting desperation on the part of those who see the uselessness and inhumanity of the war, together with an increasing stubbornness and truculence on the part of those who insist they want to win, regardless of what victory may mean.

What will the situation be when this book appears in print? Will the 1968 presidential election force the issue one way or another? Will the candidates *have to* make sense out of this in spite of everything? We are getting to the point where American "victory" in Vietnam is becoming a word without any possible human meaning. What matters is the ability and willingness to arrive at some kind of workable solution that will save the identity of the nation that still wants to survive in spite of us, in spite of Communism, in spite of the international balance of power. This cannot be arrived at unless the United States is willing to deescalate, stop bombing the North, stop destroying crops, and recognize the NLF as among those with whom we have to deal if we want to make peace. Obviously a perfect solution is impossible but some solution can be realized and lives can be saved.

It is still possible to learn something from Vietnam: and above all we should recognize that the United States has received from no one the mission to police every country in the world or to decide for them how they are to live. No single nation has the right to try to run the world according to its own ideas. One thing is certain, the Vietnam war is a tragic error and, in the words of the resigned volunteers, "an overwhelming atrocity."

How do we explain such atrocities? Obviously, they are well-meant and the Americans who support the war are, for the most part, convinced that it is an inescapable moral necessity. Why? For one thing, as the more sophisticated reader is well aware, the picture of the war given by the mass media and the official version of what is happening are both extremely one-sided and oversimplified, to say the least. Some claim that the public has been deliberately mis-informed. In any case, Americans do not seem to realize what effect the war is really having. The hatred of America which it is causing everywhere (analogous to the hatred of Russia after the violent suppression of the Hungarian revolt in 1956) is not just the result of Red propaganda. On the contrary, the Communists could never do such a fine job of blackening us as we are doing all by ourselves.

There is another, deeper source of delusion in the popular mythology of our time. One example of this popular mythology is examined in the first chapter of this section. It is the myth that all biological species in their struggle for survival must follow a law of aggression in which the stronger earns the right to exist by violently exterminat-ing all his competitors. This pseudoscientific myth is simply another version of the cliché that "might makes right" and of course it was explicitly used and developed by the ideologists of Nazism. This canonization of violence by pseudoscience has come to be so much taken for granted, that when Konrad Lorenz in his carefully thought out study *On Aggression* sought to qualify it in very important ways, his book has simply been lumped with others, like Mr. Ardrey's, as one more rationalization of the aggression theory. Thus in *The New York Times Book Review* (Christmas issue, 1967) the paperback edition of *On Aggression* is summarized with approval in this one line: "Like all other animals man is instinctively aggressive." True, of course, up to a point. But this contains the same implicit false con-clusion ("therefore he *has to* beat up and destroy members of his own kind") and explicitly ignores the real point of Lorenz's book. The point is that man is the *only species*, besides the rat, who wantonly and cruelly turns on his own kind in *unprovoked* and murderous hostility. Man is the only one who deliberately seeks to *destroy* his own kind (as opposed to merely resisting encroachment).

To quote a prominent Dutch psychoanalyst who, among other things, has studied the mentality of Nazi war criminals:

> What we usually call hatred or hostility is different from normal self-assertive aggression. The former are hypercharged fantasy products, mixed with reactions to frustrations. They form an aura of intense anticipation of revenge and greater discharge in the future. . . . This finds its most paradoxical action in the hatred of those who want to break out into history. They destroy because they want to be remembered. NO OTHER ANIMAL AVAILS HIMSELF OF PLANS FOR MOBILIZATION AND FUTURE ATTACK. However, man gets caught in his own trap, and what he once dreamed up in a fatal hour often takes possession of him so that he is finally compelled to act it out.[1]

Now this develops the point made by Lorenz in *On Aggression*. Lorenz *distinguishes* the destructive hostility of men and of rats from the natural self-assertive aggression common to all species, and indicates that far from pointing to the "survival of the fittest" this drive toward intraspecific aggression may perhaps lead to the self-destruction of the human race. That is the thesis developed in detail by Dr. Meerloo. Mr. Ardrey's book, like so much other popular mythology on the subject, serves to contribute to those "hypercharged fantasies" by which modern man at once excuses and foments his inner hostilities until he is compelled to discharge them, as we are now doing, with immense cost for innocent and harmless people on the other side of the globe.[2]

It is because of these obsessions and fantasies that we continue to draft our young men into the army when in fact a professional army of enlisted men would suffice, along with our fabulous nuclear arsenal, to meet any conceivable need for national defense. The Vietnam war has called the legality and justice of the draft law into question, and rightly. Our young men feel that they are simply being imposed upon and that their lives are being stupidly sacrificed, not to defend the country but to act out the manias of politicians and manufacturers who think they have a mission to police the world and run the affairs of smaller countries in the interests of American business. The draft law ought to be abolished. That would somewhat lessen the temptation

1. I am grateful to my friend Dr. Joost A. M. Meerloo for permission to quote from his unpublished manuscript of the English version of *Homo Militants*.
2. I have examined elsewhere the psychological connection between the Indian wars of extermination in the last century, and the Vietnam war. See: "Ishi: A Meditation," in the *Catholic Worker*, March, 1967.

to get involved in any more "overwhelming atrocities" like the one in Vietnam.

Part Three: From Nonviolence to Black Power

Violence is as American as cherry pie.
(H. Rap Brown)

The Nonviolent Civil Rights movement has practically ceased to exist. The nonviolent struggle for integration was won on the law books—and was lost in fact. Integration is more myth than real possibility. The result has been that nonviolence both as tactic and as mystique has been largely rejected as irrelevant by the American Negro. At the same time, the struggle for racial recognition has taken on an entirely new and more aggressive character.

First of all, Frantz Fanon has replaced Martin Luther King as the prophet of Black America, and Malcolm X has become its martyr. Fanon was a black psychoanalyst from the French colony of Martinique. He joined in the Algerian conflict and preached a mystique of violence as necessary for the Third World to recover its identity and organize for revolutionary self-liberation. The Black Power movement in America has accepted this doctrine as simpler, and more effective, and more meaningful than Christian nonviolence.

It must be admitted that for the majority of black Americans, Christian nonviolence remained highly ambiguous. The Negro felt himself imprisoned in the fantasy image of him devised by the white man: an image of subservient, subhuman, passive tutelage and minority. Part of this image was the assumption that the Negro was there to be beaten over the head. Whether he chose to accept his beating with Christian dignity and herioc, self-sacrificial motives was a matter of supreme indifference to people like Bull Connor.

It is true that the Montgomery bus strike and the Birmingham demonstrations did communicate to the whole nation an image of Negro dignity, maturity and integrity—an example of restraint and nobility which should not have been lost on a culture with our professed ideals. It was unfortunately soon forgotten when black people in the North began to ask for open housing. Northern liberals might admire black dignity at a distance, but they still did not want all that nobility right next door: it might affect property values. Nobility is one thing and property values quite another.

Second, the Vietnam war has had a great deal to do with the new trend to Black Power. The Negroes have been more keenly aware than anyone else of the war's ambiguities. They have tended to identify themselves with the Vietnamese—indeed with the Vietcong—and have not paid much heed to the official rhetoric of Washington. They have. on the contrary, seen the Vietnam war as another manifestation of

Whitey's versatility in beating down colored people. They have naturally concluded that white America is not really interested in nonviolence at all.

Rap Brown's statement that "violence is as American as cherry pie" is steeped in the pungent ironies which characterize the new language or racial conflict. (One is tempted to explore possible psychoanalytic insights in the droll image used. Orality, mother love, hate of brother . . .) Yes, violence is thoroughly American and Rap Brown is saying that it is in fact the real American language. Perhaps so, perhaps not. But in any event, it is the language the Black American has now elected to speak. Oddly enough, he instantly got himself a much better hearing when he did so.

America sat up and began paying a great deal of attention. "Black Power" became an explosive and inexhaustible theme in the white media. It turned out to be a much better money-maker than nonviolence (indeed nonviolence was found to interest the American public only insofar as it could be seen as an obscure, perverse form of violence— a dishonest and so to speak "inverted" violence—hence the persistent snide allusions attempting to link nonviolence with passivity and homosexuality). Black Power was clearly a message that somehow white America *wanted* to hear. Not of course that white America was not scared, it was deliciously afraid. And glad. Because now things were so much simpler. One had perfectly good reasons to call out the cops and the National Guard.

Well, the blacks wanted it that way too. It was also simpler for them. And they turned it into a self-justifying weapon. There is a lot of truth in this arraignment of white America by Rap Brown:

> You sit out there and you pretend violence scares you, but you watch TV every night and you can't turn it on for five minutes without seeing somebody shot to death or karated to death. Violence is part of your culture. There's no doubt about it. You gave us violence and this is the only value that black people can use to their advantage to end oppression. . . . Johnson says every day if Vietnam don't come round, Vietnam will burn down. I say that if America don't come round America should be burned down. *It's the same thing.*

My reason for quoting these lines is not necessarily to approve a program of arson, but to make the point that it is, quite literally *the same thing* and to congratulate Rap Brown on the firm and acute justice of his ironic insight.

An America that destroys Vietnamese noncombatants with napalm has no right to object when blacks at home burn down their slums. Indeed, if there is a difference, it is that the second case is more justifiable than the first: it is a protest against real injustice.

It is perfectly logical that the America of LBJ should be at once the

America of the Vietnam war and the Detroit riots. It's the same America, the same violence, the same slice of mother's cherry pie. (Or maybe it's mammy's pie, I don't know).

The people who have been most shocked by the Black Power movement are the white liberals. And of course they are right, because the whole impact of the movement is directed against *them*. It is a rejection of their tender and ambiguous consciences, their taste for compromise, their desire to eat momma's cherry pie and still have it, their semiconscious proclivity to use the Negro for their own sentimental, self-justifying ends. The black man has definitely seen through and summarily rejected the white liberal. The overtones of racism in the Black Power program are, in their way, an acknowledgment that the Negro feels the white segregationist to be more honest, in his way, than the liberal. Of course this infuriates the liberal, because it is supposed to do just that. And for that reason it is not to be taken too seriously.

The Black Power movement is not just racism in reverse. This racist suggestion is of course a built-in ambiguity which is at once a strength and a weakness of the movement. For two reasons it has to *appear* racist: to help the black man consolidate his sense of identity, and to rebuff the sentimental and meddling integrationism of the white liberal. There is also a third reason: to get the liberals off the black man's back, and to make it quite clear that the Negro wants to run his own liberation movement from now on, without being told what to do by someone who cannot really understand his situation. If the white liberal wants to help, let him do so indirectly. Let him help poor whites, and let him try to show poor whites that they have much the same problems as the blacks, and that they therefore should not mess with the blacks or oppose them.

It is of course to the interests of white society and in particular of the white mass media to confuse and mishandle the whole Black Power issue. The more it can be treated as an eruption of berserk violence and African bloodlust the better the story will be and the more the white public will be charmed into gooseflesh by it. The frank exploitation of this sensationalist aspect of the race crisis is illustrated by the way *Esquire* got William Worthy to write on Black Power and then, against his will, gave his contribution a highly slanted and misleading publicity campaign (emphasizing "racist" implications). For which Worthy then sued the magazine.

This wilful distortion and exploitation make it completely impossible for the average reader to be properly informed about Black Power. He is predisposed to violent and panic reactions, and it can be said that the whole of America is now primed for an explosion of anarchic destructiveness and aimless slaughter. The fault does not lie with Black Power, or not entirely. The Black Power movement has simply elected to act as catalyst, in order that what is deeply hidden in American society may come out into the open. And evidently it will.

The essays that follow cannot pretend to be anything like adequate to the present situation. The first one is by now completely dated: it represents a provisional view of things in 1964. The one on the summer of 1967 is also provisional, but a few sentences here may serve to retrace the same outlines with firmer and more definite strokes, thanks to better information and to more mature reflection.

The Black Power movement is not really a racist movement, but it is definitely revolutionary. As Rap Brown says, again: "We are not an anti-white movement, we are anti-anybody who is anti-black." It is a frankly violent movement. It is an antiliberal movement, because it takes as axiomatic the belief that liberals are in favor of the established power institutions and of all liberal ideologies which covertly or otherwise aim at preserving these. Black Power claims it wants to destroy white institutions but in this it is perhaps ambiguous. Doubtless there are many in the Black Power movement who are frankly revolutionary, and passionately desire to destroy the American capitalist system. Others, on the other hand, are already moving toward more sophisticated (or more corrupt?) establishment positions, and are accused of careerism, of professorial rhetoric, and of complicity with the government-supported intellectuals. In fact they are accused of *becoming* establishment intellectuals. It is not my place here to say whether or not this is true, but it is obviously a familiar development. It is altogether possible that the American establishment will be smart enough to neutralize Black Power by simply sucking the leaders into the government or academic machine, as was done before with the older and less radical Negro organizations. The question then is: how long before Rap Brown becomes another Uncle Tom?

The Black Power movement is explicitly identified with and involved in the world revolutionary ferment in the Third World. "We are members of the Third World." "The liberation of oppressed people across the world depends on the liberation of black people in this country."

Is Black Power a Marxist movement? No. At least not yet. In fact, the danger of the leaders being sucked into a Marxist establishment is just as great as that of their being absorbed by the American establishment. In either case Black Power will become a white movement again —dominated by white ideologies, plugged in to a white tradition. In which case it will be neutralized in a different way.

Black Power thus claims to be relevant not only to American black people but to people of all colors, everywhere, who are held down in tutelage and subservience by the big white powers—whether American, European or Russian. It claims to be relevant also to the dissatisfied and disengaged within U.S. society (the hippies). *It is part of a world movement of refusal and rejection of the value system we call Western culture.* It is therefore at least implicitly critical of Christianity as a white man's religion and accepts Christianity only as somewhat radically revised: "Christ was (literally and historically) a black man!" (Actually, there is a certain typological point to this, but I cannot discuss it here).

What is to be said about Black Power? What does it mean to a serious—therefore radical—Christian? I for one do not believe a radical Christian has a moral obligation to manufacture Molotov cocktails in the cellar and smuggle them into the ghetto. Nor do I believe he has a moral obligation to convert the Black Power movement back to nonviolence (which is unlikely anyhow).

I do believe that the Christian is obligated, by his commitment to Christ, to seek out effective and authentic ways of peace in the midst of violence. But merely to demand support and obedience to an established disorder which is essentially violent through and through will not qualify as "peacemaking."

There are no easy and simple solutions to this problem, but in the long run the evil root that has to be dealt with is the root of violence, hatred, poison, cruelty and greed which is part of the system itself. The job of the white Christian is then partly a job of diagnosis and criticism, a prophetic task of finding and identifying the injustice which is the cause of *all* the violence, both white and black, which is also the root of war, and of the greed which keeps war going in order that some might make money out of it.

The delicacy and difficulty of the task are due, of course, to the fact that, in spite of all good intentions, Christians themselves have at times come to identify this evil of greed and power with "Christian order." They have confused it with peace, with right, with justice and with freedom, not distinguishing what really contributes to the good of man and what simply panders to his appetite for wealth and power.

We do not have to go and burn down the slums: but perhaps we might profitably consider whether some of our own venerable religious institutions are not, without our realizing it, supporting themselves in part by the exploitation of slum real estate, or capitalizing in some other way on a disastrous and explosive situation.

In any case, we have to make a clear decision. Black Power or no Black Power, I for one remain *for* the Negro. I trust him, I recognize the overwhelming justice of his complaint, I confess I have no right whatever to get in his way, and that as a Christian I owe him support, not in his ranks but in my own, among the whites who refuse to trust him or hear him, who want to destroy him.

Part Four: Violence and the Death of God: Or God as Unknown Soldier

Since the essays in this section spell out some of the things I have against the "Death of God" theology, it is only fair that I begin by saying what I think can be said *for* it.

First of all, the radical "Death of God" theologians are not only to

be taken very seriously as Christians, but they are characteristic products of a real theological revival. The present time, for all its confusions
and ambiguities, is certainly one of theological ferment: it is one of
the most active periods in the history of theological thought. This
fruitfulness and creativity have been due largely to men like Karl
Barth, Paul Tillich, Karl Rahner, Jacques Maritain, Rudolf Bultmann
and the other well-known names of the first half of the century. There
are many others appearing on all sides after the Council. The Honest
to God set in England is perhaps overly naïve, and it is their popular
theology that I have tended to question most. In America, there is no
coherent, still less unanimous, Death of God movement. There is quite
a lot of variety in the thinking of Altizer (often hard to follow),
Hamilton (apostle of the Playboy type) and Vahanian, a serious
iconoclast with whom I tend most consistently to agree. In what fol-
lows, I am considering the "Death of God" chiefly from the viewpoint
of Vahanian.

The basic premise of the Death of God theology is not, of course, the
old and outworn scientific atheism of the nineteenth century. For this
radical theology, the whole question of God's objective existence is
completely irrelevant. The approach is altogether different: man's
capacity to experience and to apprehend religious thought and concepts of God. Traditional theology has tended to assume that man
experienced in himself a need for ultimate certitude which could only
be satisfied by God's manifestation of himself in revealed truth. The
Death of God starts by taking it as axiomatic that no modern man in
good faith can really have an authentic religious experience that is not
an experience of God's *absence*. Traditional theology posits God's
hidden presence and works to make that presence manifest. In the
light of God's presence and of his love, everything else becomes clear.
God is the key to everything. The Death of God theology begins with
a claim that this whole approach has utterly failed: to argue that man
feels in himself a need for God, to go on to speak of the presence of
God, and to explain everything else in this light is, it believes, simply to
substitute ideas about God for gratuitously assumed "presence" of God
and thus to make him all the more inexorably absent. In other words,
it is not only that traditional theology proves nothing, but it antagonizes
and alienates modern man and makes it all the more difficult for him
to find any meaning whatever in the concept of God.

Now this is no new or revolutionary discovery. The approach to
God "as unknown" has always had a recognized place in Catholic
theology, and Protestantism also asserted from the beginning that a
too sophisticated intellectual and rational structure in theology might
neutralize the living and personal encounter with the inscrutable God
of revelation in faith. Traditional theology itself has always recognized
the insufficiency of propositions *about* God and *about* redemption
which tend to objectify God and set him off at arm's length so that he
can be "used" and "manipulated." Such a god becomes completely

unreal—a mere convenience, serving man's purposes, a social commodity, a cosmic tranquillizer to be packaged and marketed along with any other product. The Death of God is a necessary iconoclastic protest against every form of popular religion which has blasphemed God by trying to sell him on the same terms as next year's Chevrolet.

Furthermore, the accusation runs (and I run right with it), this conceptualizing of God has tended more and more to identify the God of the Bible and of the Church with the Angel of the West—the Power or principality which is the "Guiding Spirit" of European-American civilization. The hidden God "whom no man shall see and live" and whose only manifestation is "in Christ" has been claimed as visible and present in the spirit, the ethos, the inner drive and the whole cultural outlook of the Western world. Thus the ways and attitudes of the post-Roman, medieval, then Renaissance, then enlightenment, then technological West have come to be seen as the vesture and even as the Face of God. Europe and America became the only true locus of his epiphany. Western man became in fact the manifestation of God in and as Christ. Hence the whole problem of the salvation of the world could be reduced to the task of turning everybody else into a more or less plausible replica of Western man. More grossly, to make Africa Christian, one needed only to make it Belgian, German, English, French. More grossly still, to save the soul of the African one needed only to baptize him and enslave him, thus killing two birds with one stone: gaining black souls for heaven and making a fortune out of Alabama cotton.

In other words, the saving knowledge of God in Christ was simply a matter of incorporation, however rudimentary, in some limb of Western "Christian" culture. Obviously the Church was not conscious of doing this, and the tension between Church and culture, Church and state, Church and world, was always maintained at least in theory. But how real was that tension? In actual fact, while "the world" was habitually and consistently denigrated, at least in words, the tension between it and the Church was more and more relaxed. In proportion as the world proved itself able to get along without the Church, the Church became less and less demanding, Christianity issued less and less of a challenge, until finally the Church would allow you practically anything as long as you continued to obey and to conform. A few difficult and symbolic issues like birth control, clerical celibacy, one permanent marriage, remained longer than any other, but are now being corroded away too. More and more the demands of the Church resolved themselves into demands for formal and exterior gestures of pious allegiance to God alone with rather more firm commitments to the claims of Caesar.

The clearest example of this has been in war. The French revolution put the Church in a new position *vis-à-vis* the state. The state now became hostile and demanding. The position of the Church was increasingly defensive—a matter of difficult concordats which guaranteed at least the integrity of the Church *as institution.* In order to protect these guarantees, the faithful had to be ready to meet the demands of the state in other areas. The State was now in need of larger armies. Conscription was becoming more and more universal. Even clerics, even religious, exempt by their very vocation to follow the counsels of perfection, were required to waive that exemption, when necessary to protect the interests of the Church institution in an anticlerical nation (such as France). In other words, one of the ways in which the Church protected her institutional structures in potentially hostile countries was to support the nation in its wars.

One of the few real demands for heroic sacrifice still made by the Church was that the faithful put aside their scruples and fears and obey the nation without question when it summoned them to go to war, even against other supposedly "Christian" nations. Theirs not to reason why. The government knew best. They did not have to inquire too minutely into the causes of the war or into the ways by which it was being waged. Suffice it that the bishops, by their approval, implied that the war and everything about it was "just." And the bishops, in their turn, as good patriots, left all these technicalities to the Ministry of War.

Thus it happened that the Christian gave heroic witness to his God and his faith by a meek, unquestioning obedience even unto death in submission to a Church authority that ordered him to submit to a civil authority that was not necessarily Christian—perhaps even anti-Christian.

Thus in fact God was drafted into all the armies and invited to get out there and kill himself.

As far as Europe was concerned, these rites were already thoroughly solemnized in World War I, but the Second World War guaranteed their full and complete efficacy. The nihilism and black despair of French literary and atheistic existentialism after World War II gave conclusive evidence that God had been a casualty of the war. He had died in it as one—or all—of its soldiers, both known and unknown. For the United States—which underwent a brief spasm of popular religion after World War II—the immolation has proceeded in Korea and most especially in Vietnam.

The effect of this more or less complete identification of God with "Western civilization" and with "Western society" regarded as still implicitly Christian has been of course that the crisis of Western civilization has also been necessarily a crisis of Christianity and of Christian faith. In this crisis, the Christian position has been one of more and more intolerable ambiguity, since in fact the last remaining elements of Christianity in Western culture have all but bled away.

The reaction of Christians has been somewhat frantic—where there has been any real reaction at all. One tended to lash out wildly against "materialism" and "secularism" and other scapegoat ideas, and to adopt a rather rigid posture of belief in order to maintain some coherent sense of Christian identity. But now that theologians and churchmen themselves are celebrating the praises of matter and of the secular city, this identity has been further undermined.

The true believers in this state of insecurity and frustration have only manifested more clearly and more pitifully the contradiction of their inner state. They have come out vociferously for the most bizarre, the most fanatical, the most aberrant causes in politics and culture. You can now find the most ardent Christians lined up in the most ridiculous, regressive, irrational parades. If they were concerned only with flying saucers and conversations with the departed it would not be so bad: but they are also deeply involved in racism, in quasi-Fascist nationalism, in every shade of fanatical hate cult, and in every semilunatic pressure group that is all the more self-congratulatory in that it is supported by the affluent as well as by the clergy. Such Christianity is of course a mere monstrosity and tends to make us believe that our Christian institutions are, in Vahanian's words, only "the lips with which we praise God while our hearts are far from him." He says:

> The survival of the Christian tradition is handicapped rather than helped by the existence of structures that are Christian in name only. It was doubtless easier to make the conversion from pre-Christian to Christian than it is from post-Christian to Christian. . . .
>
> Ultimately, organized religion, with its variegated paraphernalia, by trying to show how pertinent faith is, blunts it and mummifies it; [this leads to] the cultural annexation of God or a deliquescence of faith into religiosity. . . .
>
> (*Wait Without Idols*)

In such a situation, who needs atheists? The unbelief of believers is amply sufficient to make God repugnant and incredible.

Here we have to take account of the positive Christian affirmation made by the Death of God theologians. It is this: the deformation of God, due to the manipulative exploitation of him in the official concepts, is self-destroying. "God is man's failure." The intentness with which official Christianity seeks to make God relevant to man makes him so irrelevant that there remains but one alternative: to declare him dead. Then the true God, the God who is "absent," comes to life again.

When the god invented by man "dies" (he never really lived) then the true God is once again mysteriously present precisely because "God is absent." For Vahanian, Biblical religion shows us once for all that man's basic obligation to God is iconoclasm. That sounds wild, but it is only a reformulation of the first two commandments.

The chief problem of the Death of God theology as I see it is not that its language is calculatingly and consistently insulting to the

Church, nor that it deliberately makes use of near blasphemy in its contention that the official concept of God has now become blasphemous. All this can be understood when it is seen in the atmosphere of creativity and prophetism which surely is a sign of theology in our time. The real problem is that the Death of God theology too easily falls short of the prophetism to which it lays claim. It is often mere sophomoric antireligion and anticlericalism, and seems to end by subjecting man more completely and more arbitrarily to the massive domination of post-Christian secularism. My feeling is that the Death of God theology simply issues in acquiescence to political totalism, the police state—whether capitalist or Communist makes little difference. Either way, by conventional Christianity or by the Death of God, we seem to end up rendering everything to Caesar.

Nevertheless, the challenge issued by the Death of God theology is not to be evaded. In order to disentangle Christian faith from the crisis and collapse of Western culture, and open it to entirely new world perspectives, we have to be able to renounce the mighty spirit that has let himself be set up in the place of God: the Angel of the West.

Blessed Are the Meek:
The Christian Roots of Nonviolence

It would be a serious mistake to regard Christian nonviolence simply as a novel tactic which is at once efficacious and even edifying, and which enables the sensitive man to participate in the struggles of the world without being dirtied with blood. Nonviolence is not simply a way of proving one's point and getting what one wants without being involved in behavior that one considers ugly and evil. Nor is it, for that matter, a means which anyone legitimately can make use of according to his fancy for any purpose whatever. To practice nonviolence for a purely selfish or arbitrary end would in fact discredit and distort the truth of nonviolent resistance.

Nonviolence is perhaps the most exacting of all forms of struggle, not only because it demands first of all that one be ready to suffer evil and even face the threat of death without violent retaliation, but because it excludes mere transient self-interest from its considerations. In a very real sense, he who practices nonviolent resistance must commit himself not to the defense of his own interests or even those of a particular group: he must commit himself to the defense of objective truth and right and above all of *man*. His aim is then not simply to "prevail" or to prove that he is right and the adversary wrong, or to make the adversary give in and yield what is demanded of him.

Nor should the nonviolent resister be content to prove *to himself* that *he* is virtuous and right, and that *his* hands and heart are pure even though the adversary's may be evil and defiled. Still less should he seek for himself the psychological gratification of upsetting the adversary's conscience and perhaps driving him to an act of bad faith and refusal of the truth. We know that our unconscious motives may, at times, make our nonviolence a form of moral aggression and even a subtle provocation designed (without our awareness) to bring out the evil we hope to find in the adversary, and thus to justify ourselves in our own eyes and in the eyes of "decent people." Wherever there is a high moral ideal there is an attendant risk of pharisaism, and non-violence is no exception. The basis of pharisaism is division: on one hand this morally or socially privileged self and the elite to which it belongs. On the other hand, the "others," the wicked, the unenlightened, whoever they may be, Communists, capitalists, colonialists, traitors, international Jewry, racists, etc.

Christian nonviolence is not built on a presupposed division, but on the basic unity of man. It is not out for the conversion of the wicked to the ideas of the good, but for the healing and reconciliation of man with himself, man the person and man the human family.

The nonviolent resister is not fighting simply for "his" truth or for "his" pure conscience, or for the right that is on "his side." On the contrary, both his strength and his weakness come from the fact that he is fighting for *the* truth, common to him and to the adversary, *the* right which is objective and universal. He is fighting for *everybody*.

For this very reason, as Gandhi saw, the fully consistent practice of nonviolence demands a solid metaphysical and religious basis both in being and in God. This comes *before* subjective good intentions and sincerity. For the Hindu this metaphysical basis was provided by the Vedantist doctrine of the Atman, the true transcendent Self which alone is absolutely real, and before which the empirical self of the individual must be effaced in the faithful practice of *dharma*. For the Christian, the basis of nonviolence is the Gospel message of salvation for *all men* and of the Kingdom of God to which *all* are summoned. The disciple of Christ, he who has heard the good news, the announcement of the Lord's coming and of His victory, and is aware of the definitive establishment of the Kingdom, proves his faith by the gift of his whole self to the Lord in order that *all* may enter the Kingdom. This Christian discipleship entails a certain way of acting, a *politeia*, a *conservatio*, which is proper to the Kingdom.

The great historical event, the coming of the Kingdom, is made clear and is "realized" in proportion as Christians themselves live the life of the Kingdom in the circumstances of their own place and time. The saving grace of God in the Lord Jesus is proclaimed to man existentially in the love, the openness, the simplicity, the humility and the self-sacrifice of Christians. By their example of a truly Christian understanding of the world, expressed in a living and active application of the Christian faith to the human problems of their own time, Christians manifest the love of Christ for men (John 13:35, 17:21), and by that fact make him visibly present in the world. The religious basis of Christian nonviolence is then faith in Christ the Redeemer and obedience to his demand to love and manifest himself in us by a certain manner of acting in the world and in relation to other men. This obedience enables us to live as true citizens of the Kingdom, in which the divine mercy, the grace, favor and redeeming love of God are active in our lives. Then the Holy Spirit will indeed "rest upon us" and act in us, not for our own good alone but for God and his Kingdom. And if the Spirit dwells in us and works in us, our lives will be a continuous and progressive conversion and transformation in which we also, in some measure, help to transform others and allow ourselves to be transformed by and with others, in Christ.

The chief place in which this new mode of life is set forth in detail is the Sermon on the Mount. At the very beginning of this great inaugural discourse, the Lord numbers the beatitudes, which are the theological foundation of Christian nonviolence: Blessed are the poor in spirit . . . blessed are the meek (Matthew 5:3-4).

This does not mean "blessed are they who are endowed with a tranquil natural temperament, who are not easily moved to anger, who are always quiet and obedient, who do not naturally resist." Still less does it mean "blessed are they who passively submit to unjust oppression." On the contrary, we know that the "poor in spirit" are those of whom the prophets spoke, those who in the last days will be the "humble of the earth," that is to say the oppressed who have no human weapons to rely on and who nevertheless are true to the commandments of Yahweh, and who hear the voice that tells them: "Seek justice, seek humility, perhaps you will find shelter on the day of the Lord's wrath" (Sophonias 2:3). In other words they seek justice in the power of truth and of God, not by the power of man. Note that Christian meekness, which is essential to true nonviolence, has this eschatological quality about it. It refrains from self-assertion and from violent aggression because it sees all things in the light of the great judgment. Hence it does not struggle and fight merely for this or that ephemeral gain. It struggles for the truth and the right which alone will stand in that day when all is to be tried by fire (I Corinthians 3:10-15).

Furthermore, Christian nonviolence and meekness imply a particular understanding of the power of human poverty and powerlessness when they are united with the invisible strength of Christ. The Beatitudes indeed convey a profound existential understanding of the dynamic of the Kingdom of God—a dynamic made clear in the parables of the mustard seed and of the yeast. This is a dynamism of patient and secret growth, in belief that out of the smallest, weakest, and most insignificant seed the greatest tree will come. This is not merely a matter of blind and arbitrary faith. The early history of the Church, the record of the apostles and martyrs remains to testify to this inherent and mysterious dynamism of the ecclesial "event" in the world of history and time. Christian nonviolence is rooted in this consciousness and this faith.

This aspect of Christian nonviolence is extremely important and it gives us the key to a proper understanding of the meekness which accepts being "without strength" (*gewaltlos*) not out of masochism, quietism, defeatism or false passivity, but trusting in the strength of

the Lord of truth. Indeed, we repeat, Christian nonviolence is nothing
if not first of all a formal profession of faith in the Gospel message that
the *Kingdom has been established* and that the Lord of truth is indeed
risen and reigning over his Kingdom.

Faith of course tells us that we live in a time of eschatological struggle,
facing a fierce combat which marshalls all the forces of evil and darkness against the still-invisible truth, yet this combat is already decided
by the victory of Christ over death and over sin. The Christian can
renounce the protection of violence and risk being humble, therefore
vulnerable, not because he trusts in the supposed efficacy of a gentle
and persuasive tactic that will disarm hatred and tame cruelty, but
because he believes that the hidden power of the Gospel is demanding
to be manifested in and through his own poor person. Hence in perfect
obedience to the Gospel, he effaces himself and his own interests and
even risks his life in order to testify not simply to "the truth" in a
sweeping, idealistic and purely platonic sense, but to the truth that is
incarnate in a concrete human situation, involving living persons whose
rights are denied or whose lives are threatened.
  Here it must be remarked that a holy zeal for the cause of humanity
in the abstract may sometimes be mere lovelessness and indifference
for concrete and living human beings. When we appeal to the highest
and most noble ideals, we are more easily tempted to hate and contemn
those who, so we believe, are standing in the way of their realization.
  Christian nonviolence does not encourage or excuse hatred of a
special class, nation or social group. It is not merely *anti*-this or that.
In other words, the evangelical realism which is demanded of the Christian should make it impossible for him to generalize about "the wicked"
against whom he takes up moral arms in a struggle for righteousness.
He will not let himself be persuaded that the adversary is totally wicked
and can therefore never be reasonable or well-intentioned, and hence
need never be listened to. This attitude, which defeats the very purpose of nonviolence—openness, communication, dialogue—often accounts for the fact that some acts of civil disobedience merely
antagonize the adversary without making him willing to communicate
in any way whatever, except with bullets or missiles. Thomas à Becket,
in Eliot's play *Murder in the Cathedral,* debated with himself, fearing
that he might be seeking martyrdom merely in order to demonstrate
his own righteousness and the King's injustice: "This is the greatest
treason, to do the right thing for the wrong reason."

Now all these principles are fine and they accord with our Christian
faith. But once we view the principles in the light of current *facts,* a
practical difficulty confronts us. If the "gospel is preached to the poor,"
if the Christian message is essentially a message of hope and redemption
for the poor, the oppressed, the underprivileged and those who have

no power humanly speaking, how are we to reconcile ourselves to the fact that Christians belong for the most part to the rich and powerful nations of the earth? Seventeen percent of the world's population control eighty percent of the world's wealth, and most of these seventeen percent are supposedly Christian. Admittedly those Christians who are interested in nonviolence are not ordinarily the wealthy ones. Nevertheless, like it or not, they share in the power and privilege of the most wealthy and mighty society the world has ever known. Even with the best subjective intentions in the world, how can they avoid a certain ambiguity in preachng nonviolence? It this not a mystification?

We must remember Marx's accusation that "the social principles of Christianity encourage dullness, lack of self-respect, submissiveness, self-abasement, in short all the characteristics of the proletariat." We must frankly face the possibility that the nonviolence of the European or American preaching Christian meekness may conceivably be adulterated by bourgeois feelings and by an unconscious desire to preserve the status quo against violent upheaval.

On the other hand, Marx's view of Christianity is obviously tendentious and distorted. A real understanding of Christian nonviolence (backed up by the evidence of history in the Apostolic Age) shows not only that it is a *power*, but that it remains perhaps the only really effective way of transforming man and human society. After nearly fifty years of communist revolution, we find little evidence that the world is improved by violence. Let us however seriously consider at least the *conditions* for relative honesty in the practice of Christian nonviolence.

1. Nonviolence must be aimed above all at the transformation of the present state of the world, and it must therefore be free from all occult, unconscious connivance with an unjust use of power. This poses enormous problems—for if nonviolence is too political it becomes drawn into the power struggle and identified with one side or another in that struggle, while if it is totally apolitical it runs the risk of being ineffective or at best merely symbolic.

2. The nonviolent resistance of the Christian who belongs to one of the powerful nations and who is himself in some sense a privileged member of world society will have to be clearly not *for himself* but *for others*, that is for the poor and underprivileged. (Obviously in the case of Negroes in the United States, though they may be citizens of a privileged nation, their case is different. They are clearly entitled to wage a nonviolent struggle for their rights, but even for them this struggle should be primarily for *truth itself*—this being the source of their power.)

3. In the case of nonviolent struggle for peace—the threat of nuclear war abolishes all privileges. Under the bomb there is not much distinc-

tion between rich and poor. In fact the richest nations are usually the most threatened. Nonviolence must simply avoid the ambiguity of an unclear and *confusing protest* that hardens the warmakers in their self-righteous blindness. This means in fact that *in this case above all nonviolence must avoid a facile and fanatical self-righteousness,* and refrain from being satisfied with dramatic self-justifying gestures.

4. Perhaps the most insidious temptation to be avoided is one which is characteristic of the power structure itself: this fetishism of immediate visible results. Modern society understands "possibilities" and "results" in terms of a superficial and quantitative idea of efficacy. One of the missions of Christian nonviolence is to restore a different standard of practical judgment in social conflicts. This means that the Christian humility of nonviolent action must establish itself in the minds and memories of modern man not only as *conceivable* and *possible,* but as *a desirable alternative* to what he now considers the only realistic possibility: namely political technique backed by force. Here the human dignity of nonviolence must manifest itself clearly in terms of a freedom and a nobility which are able to resist political manipulation and brute force and show them up as arbitrary, barbarous and irrational. This will not be easy. The temptation to get publicity and quick results by spectacular tricks or by forms of protest that are merely odd and provocative but whose human meaning is not clear may defeat this purpose.

The realism of nonviolence must be made evident by humility and self-restraint which clearly show frankness and open-mindedness and invite the adversary to serious and reasonable discussion.

Instead of trying to use the adversary as leverage for one's own effort to realize an ideal, nonviolence seeks only to enter into a dialogue with him in order to attain, together with him, the common good of *man.* Nonviolence must be realistic and concrete. Like ordinary political action, it is no more than the "art of the possible." But precisely the advantage of nonviolence is that it has a *more Christian and more humane notion of what is possible.* Where the powerful believe that only power is efficacious, the nonviolent resister is persuaded of the superior efficacy of love, openness, peaceful negotiation and above all of truth. For power can guarantee the interests of *some men* but it can never foster the good of *man.* Power always protects the good of some at the expense of all the others. Only love can attain and preserve the good of all. Any claim to build the security of *all* on force is a manifest imposture.

It is here that genuine humility is of the greatest importance. Such humility, united with true Christian courage (because it is based on trust in God and not in one's own ingenuity and tenacity), is itself a way of communicating the message that one is interested only in truth and in the genuine rights of others. Conversely, our authentic interest in the common good above all will help us to be humble, and to distrust our own hidden drive to self-assertion.

5. Christian nonviolence, therefore, is convinced that the manner in which the conflict for truth is waged will itself manifest or obscure the truth. To fight for truth by dishonest, violent, inhuman, or unreasonable means would simply betray the truth one is trying to vindicate. The absolute refusal of evil or suspect means is a necessary element in the witness of nonviolence.

As Pope Paul said before the United Nations Assembly in 1965, "Men cannot be brohers if they are not humble. No matter how justified it may appear, pride provokes tensions and struggles for prestige, domination, colonialism and egoism. In a word *pride shatters brotherhood*." He went on to say that the attempts to establish peace on the basis of violence were in fact a manifestation of human pride. "If you wish to be brothers, let the weapons fall from your hands. You cannot love with offensive weapons in your hands."

6. A test of our sincerity in the practice of nonviolence is this: are we willing to *learn something from the adversary*? If a *new truth* is made known to us by him or through him, will we accept it? Are we willing to admit that he is not totally inhumane, wrong, unreasonable, cruel, etc.? This is important. If he sees that we are completely incapable of listening to him with an open mind, our nonviolence will have nothing to say to him except that we distrust him and seek to outwit him. Our readiness to see some good in him and to agree with some of his ideas (though tactically this might look like a weakness on our part), actually gives us power: the power of sincerity and of truth. On the other hand, if we are obviously unwilling to accept any truth that we have not first discovered and declared ourselves, we show by that very fact that we are interested not in the truth so much as in "being right." Since the adversary is presumably interested in being right also, and in proving himself right by what he considers the superior argument of force, we end up where we started. Nonviolence has great power, provided that it really witnesses to truth and not just to self-righteousness.

The dread of being open to the ideas of others generally comes from our hidden insecurity about our own convictions. We fear that we may be "converted"—or perverted—by a pernicious doctrine. On the other hand, if we are mature and objective in our open-mindedness, we may find that viewing things from a basically different perspective —that of our adversary—we discover our own truth in a new light and are able to understand our own ideal more realistically.

Our willingness to take *an alternative approach* to a problem will perhaps relax the obsessive fixation of the adversary on his view, which he believes is the only reasonable possibility and which he is determined to impose on everyone else by coercion.

It is the refusal of alternatives—a compulsive state of mind which one might call the "ultimatum complex"—which makes wars in order to force the unconditional acceptance of one oversimplified interpretation of reality. This mission of Christian humility in social life is not merely to edify, but to *keep minds open to many alternatives.* The rigidity of a certain type of Christian thought has seriously impaired this capacity, which nonviolence must recover.

Needless to say, Christian humility must not be confused with a mere desire to win approval and to find reassurance by conciliating others superficially.

7. Christian hope and Christian humility are inseparable. The quality of nonviolence is decided largely by the purity of the Christian hope behind it. In its insistence on certain human values, the Second Vatican Council, following *Pacem in Terris,* displayed a basically optimistic trust *in man himself.* Not that there is not wickedness in the world, but today trust in God cannot be completely divorced from a certain trust in man. The Christian knows that there are radically sound possibilities in every man, and he believes that love and grace always have the power to bring out those possibilities at the most unexpected moments. Therefore if he has hopes that God will grant peace to the world it is because he also trusts that man, God's creature, is not basically evil: that there is in man a potentiality for peace and order which can be realized provided the right conditions are there. The Christian will do his part in creating these conditions by preferring love and trust to hate and suspiciousness. Obviously, once again, this "hope in man" must not be naïve. But experience itself has shown, in the last few years, how much an attitude of simplicity and openness can do to break down barriers of suspicion that had divided men for centuries.

It is therefore very important to understand that Christian humility implies not only a certain wise reserve in regard to one's own judgments—a good sense which sees that we are not always necessarily infallible in our ideas—but it also cherishes positive and trustful expectations of others. A supposed "humility" which is simply depressed about itself and about the world is usually a false humility. This negative, self-pitying "humility" may cling desperately to dark and apocalyptic expectations, and refuse to let go of them. It is secretly convinced that only tragedy and evil can possibly come from our present world situation. This secret conviction cannot be kept hidden. It will manifest itself in our attitudes, in our social action and in our protest. It will show that in fact we despair of reasonable dialogue with anyone. It will show that we expect only the worst. Our action seeks only to block or frustrate the adversary in some way. A protest that from the start declares itself to be in despair is hardly likely to have valuable results. At best it provides an outlet for the personal frustrations of the one protesting. It enables him to articulate his despair in public. This is not the function of Christian nonviolence. This pseudo-prophetic desperation has nothing to do with the beatitudes, even the third. No blessedness has been promised to those who are merely sorry for themselves.

In résumé, the meekness and humility which Christ extolled in the Sermon on the Mount and which are the basis of true Christian non-violence are inseparable from an eschatological Christian hope which is completely open to the presence of God in the world and therefore to the presence of our brother who is always seen, no matter who he may be, in the perspectives of the Kingdom. Despair is not permitted to the meek, the humble, the afflicted, the ones famished for justice, the merciful, the clean of heart and the peacemakers. All the beati-tudes "hope against hope," "bear everything, believe everything, hope for everything, endure everything" (I Corinthians 13:7). The beati-tudes are simply aspects of love. They refuse to despair of the world and abandon it to a supposedly evil fate which it has brought upon itself. Instead, like Christ himself, the Christian takes upon his own shoulders the yoke of the Savior, meek and humble of heart. This yoke is the burden of the world's sin with all its confusions and all its problems. These sins, confusions and problems are our very own. We do not disown them.

Christian nonviolence derives its hope from the promise of Christ: "Fear not, little flock, for the Father has prepared for you a Kingdom" (Luke 12:32).

The hope of the Christian must be, like the hope of a child, pure and full of trust. The child is totally available in the present because he has relatively little to remember, his experience of evil is as yet brief, and his anticipation of the future does not extend very far. The Christian, in his humility and faith, must be as totally available to his brother, to his world, in the present, as the child is. But he cannot see the world with childlike innocence and simplicity unless his memory is cleared of past evils by forgiveness, and his anticipation of the future is hopefully free of craft and calculation. For this reason, the humility of Christian nonviolence is at once patient and un-calculating. The chief difference between nonviolence and violence is that the latter depends entirely on its own calculations. The former depends entirely on God and on His word.

At the same time the violent or coercive approach to the solution of human problems considers man in general, in the abstract, and according to various notions about the laws that govern his nature. In other words, it is concerned with man as subject to necessity, and it seeks out the points at which his nature is consistently vulnerable in order to coerce him physically or psychologically. Nonviolence on the other hand is based on that respect for the human person without which there is no deep and genuine Christianity. It is concerned with an appeal to the liberty and intelligence of the person insofar as he is able to transcend nature and natural necessity. Instead of forcing a decision upon him from the outside, it invites him to arrive freely at a decision of his own, in dialogue and cooperation, and in the presence of that truth which Christian nonviolence brings into full view by its sacrificial witness. The key to nonviolence is the willingness of the nonviolent resister to suffer a certain amount of accidental evil in order to bring about a change of mind in the oppressor and awaken him to personal openness and to dialogue. A nonviolent protest that merely seeks to gain publicity and to show up the oppressor for what he is, without opening his eyes to new values, can be said to be in large part a failure. At the same time, a non-violence which does not rise to the level of the personal, and remains confined to the consideration of nature and natural necessity, may perhaps make a deal but it cannot really make sense.

It is understandable that the Second Vatican Council, which placed such strong emphasis on the dignity of the human person and the freedom of the individual conscience, should also have strongly approved "those who renounce the use of violence in the vindication of their rights and who resort to methods of defense which are otherwise available to weaker parties too" (*Constitution on the Church in the Modern World*, n. 78). In such a confrontation between conflicting parties, on the level of personality, intelligence and freedom, instead of with massive weapons or with trickery and deceit, a fully human solution becomes possible. Conflict will never be abolished but a new way of solving it can become habitual. Man can then act according to the dignity of that adulthood which he is now said to have reached—and which yet remains, perhaps to be conclusively proved. One of the ways in which it can, without doubt, be proved is precisely this: man's ability to settle conflicts by reason and arbitration instead of by slaughter and destruction.

The distinction suggested here, between two types of thought— one oriented to nature and necessity, the other to person and freedom —calls for further study at another time. It seems to be helpful. The "nature-oriented" mind treats other human beings as objects to be manipulated in order to control the course of events and make the future for the whole human species conform to certain rather rigidly determined expectations. "Person-oriented" thinking does not lay down these draconian demands, does not seek so much to *control* as to *respond*, and to *awaken response*. It is not set on determining anyone or anything, and does not insistently demand that persons and events correspond to our own abstract ideal. All it seeks is the openness of free exchange in which reason and love have freedom of action. In such a situation the future will take care of itself. This is the truly Christian outlook. Needless to say that many otherwise serious and sincere Christians are unfortunately dominated by this "nature-thinking" which is basically legalistic and technical. They never rise to the level of authentic interpersonal relationships outside their own intimate circle. For them, even today, the idea of building peace on a foundation of war and coercion is not incongruous—it seems perfectly reasonable!

Christian Action in World Crisis

A death struggle can also be a struggle for life, a new birth. One is sometimes tempted to think the present crisis is the final sickness unto death: there is plenty of evidence that it might be so. Or perhaps it is the birth agony of a new world. Let us hope that it is. No one can dare to predict what is about to be born of our confusion, our frenzy, our apocalyptic madness. Certainly the old order is changing, but we do not know what is to come. All we know is that we see the many-crowned and many-headed monsters rising on all sides out of the deep, from the ocean of our own hidden and collective self. We do not understand them, and we cannot. We panic at the very sight of their iridescent scales, their deadly jaws that flame with nuclear fire. But they pursue us relentlessly, even into absurd little caves fitted out with battery radios and hand-operated blowers. We find no security even in the spiritual cave of forgetfulness, the anaesthesia of the human mind that finally shuts out an unbearable truth, and goes about the business of life in torpor and stoical indifference.

And yet the monsters do not have to come to life. They are not yet fully objective like the world around us. They do not have the substance which is given to things by the creative power of God: they are the spiritual emanations of our own sick and sinful being. They exist in and by us. They are from us. They cannot exist without us. They are our illusions. They are nightmares which our incredible technological skill can all too easily actualize. But they are also dreams from which we can awaken before it is too late. They are dreams which we can still, perhaps, choose not to dream.

The awful problem of our time is not so much the dreams, the monsters, which may take shape and consume us, but the moral paralysis in our own souls which leaves us immobile, inert, passive, tongue-tied, ready and even willing to succumb. The great tragedy is in the cold, silent waters of moral death which climb imperceptibly within us, blinding conscience, drowning compassion, suffocating faith and extinguishing the Spirit. The progressive extinction of conscience, of judgment and of compassion is the inexorable work of the cold war. When the work is completed, then . . .

One thing is getting to be more and more certain. The balance of terror, which dictates all the policies of the two great armed power blocs, cannot stay "balanced" much longer. It will crash. It may crash very soon. Napoleon said you cannot sit on bayonets. You have to use them, if you have them around. This is a thousand times more true of the monstrous weapons which offer an overwhelming advantage to the one who strikes first and who strikes hardest, who smashes everything the enemy has before the enemy can wake up to his danger.

The slightest false move, the most innocent miscalculation, an ill-chosen word, a misprint, a trivial failure in the mechanism of a computer, and one hundred million people evaporate, burn to death, go up in radioactive dust, or crawl about the face of the earth howling for death to release them from agony.

We are not good at resisting sin, even under the best conditions. But under the most violent provocation, under the most diabolical pressures, when we have abdicated all morality, when we have frankly gone back to the law of the jungle, how much chance is there, humanly speaking, that we can live without disaster?

Two things are clear. First, the enemy is not just one side or the other. The enemy is not just Russia, or China, or Communism, or Castro, or Khrushchev, or capitalism, or imperialism. The enemy is on both sides. The enemy is in all of us. The enemy is war itself, and the root of war is hatred, fear, selfishness, lust. Pius XII said in 1944, "If ever a generation has known in the depths of his being the cry of 'War on war' it is our own!" As long as we arm only against Russia, we are fighting for the real enemy and against ourselves. We are fighting to release the monster in our own soul, which will devour the world. We are fighting for the demon who strives to re-assert his power over mankind. We have got to arm not against Russia but against war. Not only against war, but against hatred. Against lies. Against injustice. Against greed. Against every manifestation of these things, wherever they may be found.

Yet at the same time we cannot attempt to ignore the spiritual border line that separates the nations of the West, with their Christian background, from the officially atheistic Communist bloc. We must avoid two extremes: seeing all good on our side and all evil on their side, or, on the contrary, dismissing both sides as totally evil. The fact remains that although the Communists have explicitly rejected the Christian ethical tradition, there may still remain in Communist-dominated countries strong surviving elements of that tradition. And although we of the West appeal to the Christian tradition in favor of our own cause, and do this quite legitimately, yet nevertheless there are materialistic and atheistic elements at work among us just as powerful and just as destructive of our tradition as the materialism and atheism of the official Communist ideology.

On both sides there are powerful and fanatical pressure groups dominated by their political obsessions, who drive towards nuclear war. On both sides the vast majority desire nothing but peace. The extremists on both sides are very much alike though they regard one another as opposites. The moderates on both sides also have very much in common. One sometimes wonders if the real dividing line is not to be drawn between the fanatics (whether Russian or American) and the moderate, ordinary people of both sides.

In any case the policy-makers and propagandists are more and more clearly and cynically espousing the cause of what they call "realism": that is to say an all-out preemptive nuclear attack involving mass destruction of civilians. This policy is clearly unacceptable by Christian moral standards. In effect, the extreme bellicosity which leads each of the great power blocs to depend more and more on the threat of a preemptive attack, with no limit to the megatonic impact of the nuclear weapons and no discrimination between civil and military objectives, *is equally immoral on both sides, equally inhuman and incompatible with Christian ethics.*

In this restricted sense it may indeed be possible to find the same demonic evil at work, perhaps in different degrees, on both sides. Once one adopts the policy of nuclear "realism" which is purely and simply a policy of annihilation, then one abandons the moral advantage of fighting for freedom, justice and democracy. None of these values are likely to survive an all-out nuclear war. Even if one nation manages to win such a war, the conditions will be such that social, moral and spiritual values with which we are familiar, and which we should certainly be prepared to defend with our lives, will no longer be recognizable in the moral debacle. Such at least is the belief of Pope Pius XII and of John XXIII.

The conclusion is, then, that we must defend freedom and sanity against the bellicose fanaticism of all war-makers, whether "ours" or "theirs," and that we must strive to do so not with force but with the spiritual weapons of Christian prayer and action. But this action must be at once nonviolent and decisive. Good intentions and fond hopes are not enough.

The present world crisis is not merely a political and economic conflict. It goes deeper than ideologies. It is a crisis of man's spirit. It is a great religious and moral upheaval of the human race, and we do not really know half the causes of this upheaval. We cannot pretend to have a full understanding of what is going on in ourselves and in our society. That is why our desperate hunger for clear and definite solutions sometimes leads us into temptation. We oversimplify. We seek the cause of evil and find it here or there in a particular nation, class, race, ideology, system. And we discharge upon this scapegoat all the virulent force of our hatred, compounded with fear and anguish, striving to rid ourselves of our fear by destroying the object we have arbitrarily singled out as the embodiment of all evil. Far from curing us, this is only another paroxysm which aggravates our sickness.

The moral evil in the world is due to man's alienation from the deepest truth, from the springs of spiritual life within himself, to his alienation from God. Those who realize this try desperately to persuade and enlighten their brothers. But we are in a radically different position from the first Christians, who revolutionized an essentially religious world of paganism with the message of a new religion that had never been heard of. We are on the contrary living in an irreligious world in which the Christian message has been repeated over and over until it has come to seem empty of all intelligible content to those whose ears close to the word of God even before it is uttered. Christianity is no longer identified with newness and change, but only with the static preservation of outworn structures.

This should teach us that though the words of the Gospel still objectively retain all the force and freshness of their original life, it is not enough now for us to make them known and clarify them. It is not enough to announce the familiar message that no longer seems to be news. Not enough to teach, to explain, convince. Now above all it is the time to embody Christian truth in action even more than in words. No matter how lucid, how persuasive, how logical, how profound our theological and spiritual statements may be, they are often wasted on anyone who does not already think as we do. That is why the serene and almost classic sanity of moralists exposing the traditional teaching of Catholic theologians on the "just war" is almost total loss in the general clamor and confusion of half truths, propaganda slogans, and pernicious clichés. Who will listen and agree, except another professional theologian? What influence can such statements have in preserving sanity, clear and logical though they may be?

What is needed now is the Christian who manifests the truth of the Gospel in social action, with or without explanation. The more clearly his life manifests the teaching of Christ, the more salutary will it be. Clear and decisive Christian action explains itself and teaches in a way that words never can.

What is wanted now is therefore not simply the Christian who takes an inner complacency in the words and example of Christ, but who seeks to follow Christ perfectly, not only in his own personal life, not only in prayer and penance, but also in his political commitments and in all his social responsibilities. There is little point, today, in a morality which seeks by refined casuistical reasoning to justify conduct which comes as close as possible to sin without actually sinning. Still less is it justifiable for Christian moralists to seek to justify and permit as much as possible of force and terror, in international politics and in war, instead of struggling in every way to restrain force and bring into being a positive international authority which can effectively prevent war and promote peace.

We are at a point of momentous choice. Either our frenzy of desperation will lead to destruction, or our patient loyalty to truth, to God and to our fellow man will enable us to perform the patient, heroic task of building a world that will thrive in unity and peace. At this point, Christian action will be decisive. That is why it is supremely important for us to keep our heads and refuse to be carried away by the wild projects of fanatics who seek an oversimplified and immediate solution by means of inhuman violence.

Christians have got to speak by their actions. Their political action must not be confined to the privacy of the polling booth. It must be clear and manifest to everybody. It must speak loudly and plainly the Christian truth, and it must be prepared to defend that truth with sacrifice, accepting misunderstanding, injustice, calumny, and even imprisonment or death. It is crucially important for Christians today to adopt a clear position and back it up with everything they have got. This means an unremitting fight for justice in every sphere—in labor, in race relations, in the "third world" and above all in international affairs.

This means (to adopt a current military cliché) closing the gap between our interior intentions and our exterior acts. Our social actions must conform to our deepest religious principles. Beliefs and politics can no longer be kept isolated from one another. It is no longer possible for us to be content with abstract and hidden acts of "purity of intention" which do nothing to make our outward actions different from those of atheists or agnostics.

Nor can we be content to make our highest ideal the preservation of a minimum of ethical rectitude prescribed by natural law. Too often the nobility and grandeur of natural law have been debased and deformed by the manipulations of theorists until natural law has become indistinguishable from the law of the jungle, which is no law at all. Hence those who complacently prescribe the duty of national defense on the basis of "natural law" often forget entirely the norms of justice and humanity without which no war can be permitted. Without those norms, natural law becomes mere jungle law, that is to say crime.

The Popes have repeatedly pleaded with Christian people to show themselves in all things disciples of Christ the Prince of Peace, and to embody in their lives their faith in His teaching. "All His teaching is an invitation to peace," says Pope John XXIII in the 1961 Christmas message. Deploring the ever increasing selfishness, hardness of heart, cynicism and callousness of mankind, as war becomes once again more and more imminent, Pope John says that Christian goodness and charity must permeate all the activity, whether personal or social, of every Christian. The Pontiff quotes Saint Leo the Great in a passage which contrasts natural ethics with the nonviolent ethic of the Gospel:

"To commit injustice and to make reparation—this is the prudence of the world. On the contrary, *not to render evil for evil is the virtuous expression of Christian forgiveness.*" These words, embodying the wisdom of the Church and the heart of her moral teaching, are heard without attention and complacently discussed even by Catholics.

Too often, in practice, we tend to assume that the teaching of Christian forgiveness and meekness applies only to the individual, not to nations or collectivities. The state can go to war and exert every form of violent force, while the individual expresses his Christian meekness by shouldering his gun without resistance and obeying the command to go out and kill. This is not Pope John's idea at all. He utters a solemn warning to rulers of nations: "With the authority we have received from Jesus Christ we say: *Shun all thought of force; think of the tragedy of initiating a chain reaction of acts, decisions and resentments which could erupt into rash and irreparable deeds.* You have received great powers not to destroy but to build, not to divide but to unite, not to cause tears to be shed but to provide employment and security."

Christian action is based on the Christian conscience, and conscience has to be informed by moral truth. What are the moral options open to the Catholic in regard to nuclear war? This has seldom been made clear, and it is tragic to observe that many Catholics are in a state of ignorance and confusion on some very important points. The vague statement that "a Catholic cannot be a pacifist" (a statement that requires a great deal of clear interpretation) is taken to signify that a Catholic is bound in conscience to accept passively every form of war and military force that his government may decide to use against an enemy. According to this view, a good Christian is one who shrinks from no work of violent destruction commanded by the state in war. How far that would be from the primitive idea that the good Christian normally refused military service and suffered violence in himself rather than inflicting it on others. Such a misconception could lead to the awful conclusion that a Catholic commanded by a new Hitler to operate the furnaces of another Dachau would be only "doing his duty" if he obeyed. The noble Christian concept of duty and sacrifice must not be debased to the point where the Christian becomes the passive and servile instrument of inhuman governments.

Succinctly: A Catholic is permitted to hold the following views of nuclear war:

a. Many sound theologians have taught that the traditional conditions of a just war cannot be fully realized today and that, as Pope Pius XII himself said, "the theory of war as an apt and proportionate means of solving international conflicts is now out of date." In practice, what has been called "relative pacifism" can very certainly be held and is held by many Catholics. Without rejecting the traditional teaching that a "just war" can theoretically be possible under certain well-defined conditions, this view holds that nuclear war is by its very nature beyond the limits of the traditional doctrine. This is supported by very clear statements of Cardinal Ottaviani and Pope Pius XII. Hence, though it is not the definitive "teaching of the Church" it is certainly not only a tenable doctrine but seems to be the soundest and most traditional opinion.

b. Though absolute pacifism in a completely unqualified form has been reproved, nevertheless today the pacifist standpoint pure and simple tends in practice to rejoin the above view, since a Catholic can be a pacifist in a particular case when there are very serious reasons for believing that even a limited war may be unjust, or may "escalate" to proportions which violate justice. It is to be noted that *when a war is evidently unjust* a Catholic not only *may* refuse to serve but he is *morally obliged to refuse to participate* in it.

c. Catholic tradition has always admitted the legality of a defensive war where there is a just cause, right intention and use of the right means. It is argued that a limited nuclear war for defensive purposes can fulfill the requirements of a just war, and that therefore it is right and just to possess stockpiles of nuclear weapons and to threaten retaliation for a nuclear attack. This may be and is held by many Catholics, and it is probably the majority opinion among Catholics in the United States. But it can be said that this position, while specious and reasonable in theory, becomes very dangerous when we consider the actual facts. All theologians agree that the unrestricted use of nuclear weapons for the simple purpose of annihilation of civilian centers is completely immoral. It is nothing but murder and is never permitted, any more than a nuclear preemptive strike on civilian centers would be permitted by Christian ethics.

Could a preemptive attack on the military installations of the enemy be admitted as a "just" defensive measure? To do so would seem very rash in view of the disastrous consequences of the retaliatory war that would inevitably be unleashed, and would inevitably entail the total mass destruction of great centers of population. The statement quoted above from Pope John XXIII, while not formally declaring such an action intrinsically evil, is a solemn warning not to initiate, by any form of aggression, a chain of acts of war and violence. While it may be all very well for theologians to theorize about a limited nuclear war, it is quite evident in actual practice that the international policies of both the United States and Russia are frankly built on the threat of an all-out war of annihilation.

In such a situation our Christian duty is clear. Though no Catholic is clearly obliged to adhere to a policy of immediate nuclear disarmament, whether multilateral or unilateral, he is certainly obliged to do everything he can, in his own situation, to work for peace. It is difficult to see how one can work for peace without ultimately seeking disarmament. If he holds one of the above opinions which are tenable, he becomes obliged to a course of action which will promote peace in accordance with the view he takes. If he is one who believes, as the Popes themselves seem quite clearly to believe, that a nuclear war will most probably be a completely unjust war because its destructive effects cannot be controlled, and that it is in any case unreasonable and totally undesirable, then he will be obliged to base his political activity on the belief that war must be prevented here and now, and that we must try as best we can to work for its eventual abolition. This does not mean necessarily an all-out campaign to "ban the bomb" immediately. But it certainly does mean an insistence on peaceful means of settling international disputes. If a Catholic feels himself obliged in conscience to oppose all nuclear armaments and to demand even immediate unilateral disarmament as the best way to peace, though his director of conscience may not agree with his politics he cannot forbid him to hold this view.

There are many reasons to believe that the social action of someone like Dorothy Day, who is willing to refuse cooperation even in civil defense drills and ready to go to jail for her belief in peace, is far more significantly Christian than the rather subtle and comfy positions of certain casuists. When I consider that Dorothy Day was confined to a jail cell in nothing but a light wrap (her clothes having been taken from her) and that she could only get to Mass and Communion in the prison by dressing in clothes borrowed from prostitutes and thieves in the neighboring cells, then I lose all inclination to take seriously the self-complacent nonsense of those who consider her kind of pacifism sentimental.

A Tribute to Gandhi

In 1931 Gandhi, who had been released from prison a few months before, came to London for a conference. The campaign of civil disobedience which had begun with the Salt March had recently ended. Now there were to be negotiations. He walked through the autumn fogs of London in clothes that were good for the tropics, not for England. He lived in the slums of London, coming from there to more noble buildings in which he conferred with statesmen. The English smiled at his bald head, his naked brown legs, the thin underpinnings of an old man who ate very little, who prayed. This was Asia, wise, disconcerting, in many ways unlovely, but determined upon some inscrutable project and probably very holy. Yet was it practical for statesmen to have conferences with a man reputed to be holy? What was the meaning of the fact that one could be holy, and fast, and pray, and be in jail, and be opposed to England all at the same time?

Gandhi thus confronted the England of the depression as a small, disquieting question mark. Everybody knew him, and many jokes were made about him. He was also respected. But respect implied neither agreement nor comprehension. It indicated nothing except that the man had gained public attention, and this was regarded as an achievement. Then, as now, no one particularly bothered to ask if the achievement signified something.

Yet I remember arguing about Gandhi in my school dormitory: chiefly against the football captain, then head prefect, who had come to turn out the flickering gaslight, and who stood with one hand in his pocket and a frown on his face that was not illuminated with understanding. I insisted that Gandhi was right, that India was, with perfect justice, demanding that the British withdraw peacefully and go home; that the millions of people who lived in India had a perfect right to run their own country. Such sentiments were of course beyond comprehension. How could Gandhi be right when he was *odd?* And how could I be right if I was on the side of someone who had the wrong kind of skin, and left altogether too much of it exposed?

A counter argument was offered but it was not an argument. It was a basic and sweeping assumption that the people of India were political and moral infants, incapable of taking care of themselves, backward people, primitive, uncivilized, benighted, pagan, who could not survive without the English to do their thinking and planning for them. The British Raj was, in fact, a purely benevolent, civilizing enterprise for which the Indians were not suitably grateful. . . .

Infuriated at the complacent idiocy of this argument, I tried to sleep and failed.

Certain events have taken place since that time. Within a dozen years after Gandhi's visit to London there were more hideous barbarities perpetuated in Europe, with greater violence and more unmitigated fury than all that had ever been attributed by the wildest imaginations to the despots of Asia. The British Empire collapsed. India attained self-rule. It did so peacefully and with dignity. Gandhi paid with his life for the ideas in which he believed.

As one looks back over this period of confusion and decline in the West, the cold war, and the chaos and struggle of the world that was once colonial, there is one political figure who stands out from all the rest as an extraordinary leader of men. He is radically different from the others. Not that the others did not on occasion bear witness to the tradition of which they were proud because it was Christian. They were often respectable, sometimes virtuous men, and many of them were sincerely devout. Others were at least genteel. Others, of course, were criminals. Judging by their speeches, their programs, their expressed motives were usually civilized. Yet the best that could be said of them may be that they sometimes combined genuine capability and subjective honesty. But apart from that they seemed to be the powerless victims of a social dynamic that they were able neither to control nor to understand. They never seemed to dominate events, only to rush breathlessly after the parade of cataclysms, explaining why these had happened, and not aware of how they themselves had helped precipitate the worst of disasters. Thus with all their good intentions, they were able at best to rescue themselves after plunging blindly in directions quite other than those in which they claimed to be going. In the name of peace, they wrought enormous violence and destruction. In the name of liberty they exploited and enslaved. In the name of man they engaged in genocide or tolerated it. In the name of truth they systematically falsified and perverted truth.

Gandhi on the other hand was dedicated to peace, and though he was engaged in a bitter struggle for national liberation, he achieved this by peaceful means. He believed in serving the truth by nonviolence, and his nonviolence was effective in so far as it began first within himself.

It is certainly true that Gandhi was not above all criticism; no man is. But it is evident that he was unlike all the other world leaders of his time in that his life was marked by a wholeness and a wisdom, an integrity and a spiritual consistency that the others lacked, or manifested only in reverse, in consistent fidelity to a dynamism of evil and destruction. There may be limitations in Gandhi's thought, and his work has not borne all the fruit he himself would have hoped. These are factors which he himself sagely took into account, and having reckoned with them all, he continued to pursue the course he had chosen simply because he believed it to be true. His way was no secret: it was simply to follow conscience without regard for the consequences to himself, in the belief that this was demanded of him by God and that the results would be the work of God. Perhaps indeed for a long time these results would remain hidden as God's secret. But in the end the truth would manifest itself.

What has Gandhi to do with Christianity? Everyone knows that the Orient has venerated Christ and distrusted Christians since the first colonizers and missionaries came from the West.

Western Christians often assume without much examination that this oriental respect for Christ is simply a vague, syncretistic and perhaps romantic evasion of the challenge of the Gospel: an attempt to absorb the Christian message into the confusion and inertia which are thought to be characteristic of Asia. The point does not need to be argued here. Gandhi certainly spoke often of Jesus, whom he had learned to know through Tolstoy. And Gandhi knew the New Testament thoroughly. Whether or not Gandhi "believed in" Jesus in the sense that he had genuine Christian faith in the Gospel would be very difficult to demonstrate, and it is not my business to prove it or disprove it. I think that the effort to do so would be irrelevant in any case. What is certainly true is that Gandhi not only understood the ethic of the Gospel as well, if not in some ways better, than many Christians, but he is one of the very few men of our time who applied Gospel principles to the problems of a political and social existence in such a way that his approach to these problems was *inseparably* religious and political at the same time.

He did this not because he thought that these principles were novel and interesting, or because they seemed expedient, or because of a compulsive need to feel spiritually secure. The religious basis of Gandhi's political action was not simply a program, in which politics were marshalled into the service of faith, and brought to bear on the charitable objectives of a religious institution. For Gandhi, strange as it may seem to us, political action had to be by its very nature "religious" in the sense that it had to be informed by principles of religious and philosophical wisdom. To separate religion and politics was in Gandhi's eyes "madness" because his politics rested on a thoroughly religious interpretation of reality, of life, and of man's place in the world. Gandhi's whole concept of man's relation to his own inner being and to the world of objects around him was informed by the contemplative heritage of Hinduism, together with the principles of Karma Yoga which blended, in his thought, with the ethic of the Synoptic Gospels and the Sermon on the Mount. In such a view, politics had to be understood in the context of service and worship in the ancient sense of *leitourgia* (liturgy, public work). Man's intervention in the active life of society was at the same time by its very nature *svadharma*, his own personal service (of God and man) and worship, *yajna*. Political action therefore was not a means to acquire security and strength for one's self and one's party, but a means of witnessing to the truth and the reality of the cosmic structure by making one's own proper contribution to the order willed by God. One could thus preserve one's integrity and peace, being detached from results (which are in the hands of God) and being free from the inner violence that comes from division and untruth, the usurpation of someone else's *dharma* in place of one's own *svadharma*. These perspectives lent Gandhi's politics their extraordinary spiritual force and religious realism.

The success with which Gandhi applied this spiritual force to political action makes him uniquely important in our age. More than that, it gives him a very special importance for Christians. Our attitude to politics tends to be abstract, divisive and often highly ambiguous. Political action is by definition secular and unspiritual. It has no really religious significance. Yet it is important to the Church as an institution in the world. It has therefore an *official* significance. We look to the Church to clarify principle and offer guidance, and in addition to that we are grateful if a Christian party of some sort comes to implement the program that has thus been outlined for us. This is all well and good. But Gandhi emphasized the importance of the individual person entering political action with a fully awakened and operative spiritual power in himself, the power of *Satyagraha*, nonviolent dedication to truth, a religious and spiritual force, a wisdom born of fasting and prayer. This is the charismatic and personal force of the saints, and we must admit that we have tended to regard it with mistrust and unbelief, as though it were mere "enthusiasm" and "fanaticism." This is a lamentable mistake, because for one thing it tends to short-circuit the power and light of grace, and it suggests that spiritual dedication is and must remain something entirely divorced from political action: something for the prie-dieu, the sacristy or the study, but not for the marketplace. This in turn has estranged from the Church those whose idealism and generosity might have inspired a dedicated and creative intervention in political life. These have found refuge in groups dominated by a confused pseudo-spirituality, or by totalitarian messianism. Gandhi remains in our time as a sign of genuine union of spiritual fervor and social action in the midst of a hundred pseudo-spiritual crypto-fascist, or Communist movements in which the capacity for creative and spontaneous dedication is captured, debased and exploited by false prophets.

In a time where the unprincipled fabrication of lies and systematic violation of agreements has become a matter of course in power politics, Gandhi made this unconditional devotion to truth the mainspring of his social action. Once again, the radical difference between him and other leaders, even the most sincere and honest of them, becomes evident by the fact that Gandhi is chiefly concerned with truth and with service, *svadharma*, rather than with the possible success of his tactics upon other people, and paradoxically it was his religious conviction that made Gandhi a great politician rather than a mere tactician or operator. Note that *satyagraha* is matter for a vow, therefore of worship, adoration of the God of truth, so that his whole political structure is built on this and his other vows (*Ahimsa*, etc.) and becomes an entirely religious system. The vow of *satyagraha* is the vow to die rather than say what one does not mean.

The profound significance of *satyagraha* becomes apparent when one reflects that "truth" here implies much more than simply conforming one's words to one's inner thought. It is not by words only that we speak. Our aims, our plans of action, our outlook, our attitudes, our habitual response to the problems and challenges of life "speak" of our inner being and reveal our fidelity or infidelity to ourselves. Our very existence, our life itself contains an implicit pretention to meaning, since all our free acts are implicit commitments, selections of "meanings" which we seem to find confronting us. Our very existence is "speech" interpreting reality. But the crisis of truth in the modern world comes from the bewildering complexity of the almost infinite contradictory propositions and claims to meaning uttered by millions of acts, movements, changes, decisions, attitudes, gestures, events, going on all around us. Most of all a crisis of truth is precipitated when men realize that almost all these claims are in fact without significance when they are not in great part entirely fraudulent.

Satyagraha for Gandhi meant first of all refusing to say "nonviolence" and "peace" when one meant "violence" and "destruction." However, his wisdom differed from ours in this: he knew that in order to speak truth he must rectify more than his inner *intention*. It was not enough to say "love" and *intend* love thereafter proving the sincerity of one's own intentions by demonstrating the insincerity of one's adversary. "Meaning" is not a mental and subjective adjustment. For Gandhi, a whole lifetime of sacrifice was barely enough to demonstrate the sincerity with which he made a few simple claims: that he was not lying, that he did not intend to use violence or deceit against the English, that he did not think that peace and justice could be attained through violent or selfish means, that he did genuinely believe they could be assured by nonviolence and self-sacrifice.

Gandhi's religio-political action was based on an ancient metaphysic of man, a philosophical wisdom which is common to Hinduism, Buddhism, Islam, Judaism, and Christianity: that "truth is the inner law of our being." Not that man is merely an abstract essence, and that our action must be based on logical fidelity to a certain definition of man. Gandhi's religious action is based on a religious intuition of *being* in man and in the world, and his vow of truth is a vow of fidelity to being in all its accessible dimensions. His wisdom is based on experience more than on logic. Hence the way of peace is the way of truth, of fidelity to wholeness and being, which implies a basic respect for life not as a concept, not as a sentimental figment of the imagination, but in its deepest, most secret and most fontal reality. The first and fundamental truth is to be sought in respect for our own inmost being, and this in turn implies the recollectedness and the awareness which attune us to that silence in which alone Being speaks to us in all its simplicity.

Therefore Gandhi recognized, as no other world leader of our time has done, the necessity to be free from the pressures, the exorbitant and tyrannical demands of a society that is violent because it is essentially greedy, lustful and cruel. Therefore he fasted, observed days of silence, lived frequently in retreat, knew the value of solitude, as well as of the totally generous expenditure of his time and energy in listening to others and communicating with them. He recognized the impossibility of being a peaceful and nonviolent man if one submits passively to the insatiable requirements of a society maddened by overstimulation and obsessed with the demons of noise, voyeurism and speed.

"Jesus died in vain," said Gandhi, "if he did not teach us to regulate the whole life by the eternal law of love." Strange that he should use this expression. It seems to imply at once concern and accusation. As Asians sometimes do, Gandhi did not hesitate to confront Christendom with the principles of Christ. Not that he judged Christianity, but he suggested that the professedly Christian civilization of the West was in fact judging itself by its own acts and its own fruits. There are certain Christian and humanitarian elements in democracy, and if they are absent, democracy finds itself on trial, weighed in the balance, and no amount of verbal protestations can prevent it from being found wanting. Events themselves will proceed inexorably to their conclusion. *Pacem in Terris* has suggested the same themes to the meditation of modern Europe, America and Russia. "Civilization" must learn to prove its claims by a capacity for the peaceful and honest settlement of disputes, by genuine concern for justice toward people who have been shamelessly exploited and races that have been systematically oppressed, or the historical preeminence of the existing powers will be snatched from them by violence, perhaps in a disaster of cosmic proportions.

Gandhi believed that the central problem of our time was the acceptance or the rejection of a basic law of love and truth which had been made known to the world in traditional religions and most clearly by Jesus Christ. Gandhi himself expressly and very clearly declared himself an adherent of this one law. His whole life, his political action, finally even his death, were nothing but a witness to his commitment. "IF LOVE IS NOT THE LAW OF OUR BEING THE WHOLE OF MY ARGUMENT FALLS TO PIECES."

What remains to be said? It is true that Gandhi expressly disassociated himself from Christianity in any of its visible and institutional forms. But it is also true that he built his whole life and all his activity upon what he conceived to be the law of Christ. In fact, he died for this law which was at the heart of his belief. Gandhi was indisputably sincere and right in his moral commitment to the law of love and truth. A Christian can do nothing greater than follow his own conscience with a fidelity comparable to that which Gandhi obeyed what he believed to be the voice of God. Gandhi is, it seems to me, a model of integrity whom we cannot afford to ignore, and the one basic duty we all owe to the world of our time is to imitate him in "disassociating ourselves from evil in total disregard of the consequences."

Note on Civil Disobedience
and Nonviolent Revolution

(Submitted at the request of the National Commission on the
Causes and Prevention of Violence)

---

1. I am asked to submit some remarks on "the theory and practice of civil disobedience," the implication being that this is one of the areas of "violence" which the commission is worried about. Though this is not really my field, I have done some reading in it and have formulated some ideas which have been published chiefly in books like *Seeds of Destruction*, *Faith and Violence* and *Gandhi on Non-Violence*. In these books and related articles I have studied what might be called the "classical" approach to nonviolent conflict resolution, exemplified by Mahatma Gandhi and Martin Luther King (as well as by Tolstoy, Thoreau and other precursors). This "classical" approach has the following important characteristics:

a. It is the expression of a religious humanism and seeks to apply the ideals of traditionally religious civilizations to the resolution of conflict and the solution of social problems for which conventional political means seem to have proved inadequate.

b. It claims that instead of having recourse to revolutionary violence and to the overthrow of established systems by force, a more efficacious method is to appeal to the deepest moral idealism of a civilized tradition. It is a way of reform rather than of revolution.

c. It appeals above all to the highest ethical motivations and far from advocating the violent destruction of civilized and traditional structures as such, it bases itself on a fundamental respect for social order. This means that a scrupulous distinction is made between the unjust law, pinpointed as a source of inevitable disorder, and the essential legality of structures. Thus the theory of civil disobedience in this classic context permits only disobedience of a law that has been shown to be unjust, and at the same time it affirms respect for law and order as such by accepting punishment for the act of disobedience. This aspect of civil disobedience is often overlooked.

d. In other words, the "classical" theory of nonviolence claims to respect the values and structures of civilization even more than does the establishment, which (they claim) has become involved in the routine of retaining power and making money. Classic nonviolence questions an establishment which negates civilized values while claiming to defend them and engages in corrupt dealings which in fact are the real source of conflict and disorder. Thus, rightly or wrongly, classic nonviolence seeks to defend all that is regarded as best and highest in civilization. It is essentially a religious humanism and a mystique of reform. In this lie both its strength and its weakness.

e. This classic theory of nonviolent social change is attacked vehemently both by Marxists and by professional revolutionaries committed to the use of force in the struggle for political power, and by conservative establishments. Both these oppositions seek to discredit the classic theory of nonviolence. Because of its attachment to traditional and religious values, classic nonviolence is attacked by Marxists as essentially "bourgeois" and conservative. Because of its advocation of reform and its protest against disorders, it is attacked by the establishment as "anarchy," and sinister links with Marxists are hinted at (seldom proved because they seldom exist).

2. At this present moment, 1968, we have already passed a point of crucial decision. It can be said that the classical approach to nonviolence is no longer the dominant and guiding force in radical efforts to achieve reform and conflict resolution. The events of the past few years have inexorably built up a new polarization of violent forces and those who have hitherto been disposed to nonviolence are being forced more and more toward the violent positions of extremists. This is not so much the result of their own choice as the effect of inexorable pressures: on one hand, in the area of civil rights, the trend toward militancy and the repudiation of anything savoring of nonviolent approach is more and more represented as weak and cowardly. Nevertheless, the Peace Movement is still predominantly nonviolent and although acts of civil disobedience are becoming markedly more aggressive, the Peace Movement has not committed itself to violence—and with good reason, for it would thus tend to contradict itself. Unfortunately, the increasing use of force and the numerous complaints of brutality and police repression in the effort to stifle the voice of protest against the Vietnam war are having a disastrous effect on the Peace Movement. Though by and large the Peace Movement is still made up of nonviolent, love-affirming types who place a high premium on gentleness, conciliation, mutual understanding, dialogue, etc., they are being driven to a kind of despair of traditional civilized humanistic attitudes. Some still believe in the power of love and peaceful conciliation to effect a change in the violent and hostile adversary. Others are simply becoming convinced that the police, the military and the establishment are blindly

opposed to any reasonable expression of protest, that they refuse to listen to civilized argument, that they represent essential corruption and injustice. For instance, the young people in the Peace Movement are not especially impressed by appeals to respect law and order when they believe that the Vietnam war itself is a flagrant example of illegality and contempt for international order. When they are accused of trying to "take the law into their own hands," they answer, rightly or wrongly, that this is precisely what President Johnson and the Pentagon are doing in Asia. I am not of course espousing these arguments here: I am just citing them as examples of what the young people believe to be bad faith on the part of their elders and of authority.

It is these people who are now beginning to talk revolution. I say *talk* revolution because it is almost entirely talk (as far as I can tell). But if they feel themselves continually singled out for what they conceive to be brutal, unjust, uncomprehending treatment, they will be driven more and more to identify themselves somewhat romantically with typological figures like Che Guevara. The whole psychology of this situation calls for careful study and, I might add, sympathetic study.

3. I might say quite frankly that in my opinion one of the reasons for the current swing toward violence is that the classic nonviolent position has been consistently misrepresented, misunderstood and subjected to more and more brutal repression. The people who were at first attracted to this approach have thus been disillusioned not only with the established structures but also (more tragically) with the whole civilized tradition of religious humanism. Thus they are turning more and more not only to revolution but to a new pragmatic mystique of revolutionary humanism. To put it bluntly, the kind of brutal and incomprehending repression to which they find themselves subjected, in the name of "civilized tradition," "law and order," etc., makes them more and more convinced that there is no authentic humanism that is not militantly revolutionary. In other words, they are moving more and more toward the Marxist position. They are being driven to the Marxist position by a sort of self-fulfilling prophecy. If they are beaten over the head long enough and hard enough, they will end up as full-fledged Marxists, and then the police can say, "We told you so," and everyone can start shooting with a "clear conscience." Needless to say, I regard this as tragic futility, and in my opinion it brings us closer and closer to a particular kind of totalitarian state. It may not reproduce the crude patterns of European Gestapo culture, but it will nevertheless mean the end of real democracy and freedom for the United States of America.

4. To sum up: I ask myself this rather disquieting question: Will the commission concentrate on the suppression of nonviolent protest and disregard the real murderers, the extremists and fanatics who are already explicitly committed to violence, bloodshed, murder and destruction? The assassins are not—at least not yet—to be looked for

chiefly among the rioting students and peaceniks who burn their draft cards. And the real focus of American violence is not in esoteric groups but in the very culture itself, its mass media, its extreme individualism and competitiveness, its inflated myths of virility and toughness, and its overwhelming preoccupation with the power of nuclear, chemical, bacteriological and psychological overkill. If we live in what is essentially a culture of overkill, how can we be surprised at finding violence in it? Can we get to the root of the trouble? In my opinion, the best way to do it would have been the classic way of religious humanism and nonviolence exemplified by Gandhi. That way seems now to have been closed. I do not find the future reassuring.

War and the Crisis of Language

> The Romans, to speak generally, rely
> on force in all their enterprises and
> think it incumbent upon them to carry
> out their projects in spite of all,
> and that nothing is impossible when
> they have once decided upon it.
>
> POLYBIUS

I

Long before George Steiner pointed out that the German language was one of the casualties of Naziism and World War II, Brice Parain in France had studied the "word sickness" of 1940, the mortal illness of journalese and political prose that accompanied the collapse of France. In proportion as the country itself accepted the denatured prose of Vichy—in which peace meant aggression and liberty meant oppression—it lost its identity and its capacity for valid action. It succumbed to "a full armed language without practical application." This, Parain reflected, had already happened before, in World War I, when words meant one thing in the trenches and another behind the lines.[1]

The reflections that follow are random and spontaneous insights—less of a philosopher than of a poet. For poets are perhaps the ones who, at the present moment, are most sensitive to the sickness of language—a sickness that, infecting all literature with nausea, prompts us not so much to declare war on conventional language as simply to pick up and examine intently a few chosen pieces of linguistic garbage. But of course, one does not have to be endowed with a peculiar poetic sensibility, still less with political genius, to recognize that official statements made in Washington, about the Vietnam war, for instance, are symptoms of a national—indeed worldwide—illness. Nor is it very

---

1. See Sartre's essay on Parain in *Situations I* (Paris, 1947), p. 192.

hard to see that race riots and assassinations are also symptoms of the same illness, while they are also (and this is more important) a kind of universal language. Perhaps one might better call them an anti-language, a concrete expression of something that is uttered in fire and bullets rather than in words. And this in itself expresses an acute aware-ness of the gap between words and actions that is characteristic of modern war, because it is also characteristic of political life in general.

The malaise is universal. There is no need to quote a Swedish poet to prove it. But these lines from Gunnar Ekelöf may serve as an apéritif for what is to follow. He begins his poem "Sonata For Denatured Prose" in these words:

> crush the alphabet between your teeth yawn
> vowels, the fire is burning in hell vomit and
> spit now or never I and dizziness you or never
> dizziness now or never.
>
> we will begin over.
>
> crush the alphabet macadam and your teeth
> yawn vowels, the sweat runs in hell I am dying
> in the convolutions of my brain vomit now or
> never dizziness I and you. . . .[2]

There is no need to complete the poem. It is an angry protest against contemporary, denatured language. Ironically, it declares that ordinary modes of communication have broken down into banality and decep-tion. It suggests that violence has gradually come to take the place of other, more polite, communications. Where there is such a flood of words that all words are unsure, it becomes necessary to make one's meaning clear with blows; or at least one explores this as a valid pos-sibility.

The incoherence of language that cannot be trusted and the co-herence of weapons that are infallible, or thought to be: this is the dialectic of politics and war, the prose of the twentieth century. We shall see at the end of the chapter that awareness of this fact has made a crucial difference in the racial conflict in the United States, and everywhere else.

II

Meanwhile, it is interesting to observe that religion too has reacted to the same spastic upheaval of language. I do not here refer to the phenomenon of a radical "God is Dead" theology—which in effect is

2. Gunnar Ekelöf: *Late Arrival on Earth,* Selected Poems, trans. Robert Bly & Christine Paulston (London: 1967), p. 13.

our effort to reshape the language of religion in a last-minute attempt to save it from a plague of abstractness and formalism. This phenomenon is of course important. And so much has been said about it already—perhaps a great deal more than the subject deserves. I merely want to point out, in passing, that the fifties and sixties of our century have witnessed a curious revival of *glossolalia*—"speaking in tongues." Without attempting to evaluate this as charisma, I will at least say that it is significant in a context of religious and linguistic spasm. It is in its own way an expression of a curious kind of radicalism, a reaction to a religious language that is (perhaps obscurely) felt to be inadequate. But it is also, it seems to me, a reaction to something else. Glossolalia has flowered most abundantly in the United States, in fundamentalist and Pentecostal sects of white Protestants, and perhaps most often in the South about the time of the Freedom Rides and nonviolent civil rights demonstrations. (I do not have much information on what has taken place most recently.) This was also the time when the cold war was finally building up to the Cuba Crisis and the U.S. intervention in Vietnam was about to begin. Surely there is something interesting about this. At a time when the churches were at last becoming uneasily aware of a grave responsibility to *say something* about civil rights and nuclear war, the ones who could be least expected to be articulate on such subjects (and who often had solid dogmatic prejudices that foreclosed all discussion) began to cry out in unknown tongues.

At precisely the same moment, the Roman Catholic Church was abandoning its ancient liturgical language, the medieval Latin that was unknown to most of its members, and speaking out in a vernacular that many critics found disconcertingly banal and effete. If I refer to these things, it is not in scorn or in criticism. They are simply further expressions of a universal uneasiness about *language*—a sense of anxiety lest speech become entirely deceptive and unreal.

Can this apply to glossolalia? Of course. Fundamentalist religion assumes that the "unknown language" spoken "in the Spirit" is (though unintelligible) *more real* than the ordinary tired everyday language that everybody knows too well. Whether or not one believes that simple Texas housewives can burst out in the dialects of New Guinea head-hunters, under direct inspiration from God, there is here a significant implication that ordinary language is not good enough, and that there is something else which is at once more *real* and less comprehensible. Has ordinary language somehow failed?

I do not wish to hazard all sort of incompetent guesses about something I have not studied and do not intend to study. But one thing is quite evident about this phenomenon. He who speaks in an unknown tongue can safely speak without fear of contradiction. His utterance is *definitive* in the sense that it forecloses all dialogue. As St. Paul complained, if you utter a blessing in a strange language the congregation cannot answer "Amen" because it does not know it has been blessed.

Such utterance is so final that nothing whatever can be done about it.[3]
I wish to stress this unconscious aspiration to *definitive* utterance, to
which there can be no rejoinder.

III

Now let us turn elsewhere, to the language of advertisement, which at
times approaches the mystic and charismatic heights of glossolalia.
Here too, utterance is final. No doubt there are insinuations of dialogue,
but really there is no dialogue with an advertisement, just as there was
no dialogue between the sirens and the crews they lured to disaster on
their rocks. There is nothing to do but be hypnotized and drown, unless
you have somehow acquired a fortunate case of deafness. But who can
guarantee that he is deaf enough? Meanwhile, it is the vocation of the
poet—or anti-poet—*not* to be deaf to such things but to apply his ear
intently to their corrupt charms. An example: a perfume advertisement
from *The New Yorker* (September 17, 1966).

I present the poem as it appears on a full page, with a picture of a
lady swooning with delight at her own smell—the smell of *Arpège*.
(Note that the word properly signifies a sound—*arpeggio*. Aware that
we are now smelling music, let us be on our guard!)

> *For the love of Arpège . . .*
> *There's a new hair spray!*
>   *The world's most adored fragrance*
> *now in a hair spray. But not hair spray*
> *as you know it.*
>
>   *A delicate-as-air-spray*
>   *Your hair takes on a shimmer and sheen*
> *that's wonderfully young.*
>   *You seem to spray new life and bounce*
> *right into it. And a coif of Arpège has*
> *one more thing no other hair spray has.*
>   *It has Arpège.*

One look at this masterpiece and the anti-poet recognizes himself
beaten hands down. This is beyond parody. It must stand inviolate in
its own victorious rejection of meaning. We must avoid the temptation
to dwell on details: interior rhyme, suggestions of an esoteric cult (the
use of our product, besides making you young again, is also a kind of
gnostic initiation), of magic (our product gives you a hat of smell—
a "coif"—it clothes you in an aura of music-radiance-perfume). What
I want to point out is the logical *structure* of this sonata: is is a fool-
proof tautology, locked tight upon itself, impenetrable, unbreakable,

3. See I Corinthians 14.

irrefutable. It is endowed with a finality so inviolable that it is beyond debate and beyond reason. Faced with the declaration that "Arpège has Arpège," reason is reduced to silence (I almost said despair). Here again we have an example of speech that is at once totally trivial and totally definitive. It has nothing to do with anything real (although of course the sale of the product is a matter of considerable importance to the manufacturer!), but what it says, it says with utter finality.

The unknown poet might protest that he (or she) was not concerned with truth alone but also with beauty—indeed with love. And obviously this too enters into the structure and substance (so to speak) of the text. Just as the argument takes the form of a completely self-enclosed tautological cliché, so the content, the "experience," is one of self-enclosed narcissism woven of misty confusion. It begins with the claim that a new hair spray exists solely for love of itself and yet also exists for love of *you,* baby, because you are somehow subtly identified with Arpège. This perfume is so magic that it not only makes you smell good, it "coifs" you with a new and unassailable identity: it is you who are unassailable because it is you who have somehow become a tautology. And indeed we are reminded that just as Arpège is—or has—Arpège, so, in the popular psychology of women's magazines, "you are eminently lovable because you are just *you.*" When we reflect that the ultimate conceptions of theology and metaphysics have surfaced in such a context—hair spray—we no longer wonder that theologians are tearing their hair and crying that God is dead. After all, when every smell, every taste, every hissing breakfast food is endowed with the transcendental properties of being . . . But let us turn from art, religion, and love to something more serious and more central to the concerns of our time: war.

IV

A classic example of the contamination of reason and speech by the inherent ambiguity of war is that of the U.S. major who, on February 7, 1968, shelled the South Vietnamese town of Bentre "regardless of civilian casualties . . . to rout the Vietcong." As he calmly explained, "It became necessary to destroy the town in order to save it." Here we see, again, an insatiable appetite for the tautological, the definitive, the *final.* It is the same kind of language and logic that Hitler used for his notorious "final solution." The symbol of this perfect finality is the circle. An argument turns upon itself, and the beginning and end get lost: it just goes round and round its own circumference. A message comes in that someone thinks there might be some Vietcong in a certain village. Planes are sent, the village is destroyed, many of the people are killed. The destruction of the village and the killing of the people earn for them a final and official identity. The burned huts become "enemy structures"; the dead men, women, and children become

"Vietcong," thus adding to a "kill ratio" that can be interpreted as "favorable." They were thought to be Vietcong and were therefore destroyed. By being destroyed they became Vietcong for keeps; they entered "history" definitively as our enemies, because we wanted to be on the "safe side," and "save American lives"—as well as Vietnam.

The logic of "Red or dead" has long since urged us to identify destruction with rescue—to be "dead" is to be saved from being "Red." In the language of melodrama, our grandparents became accustomed to the idea of a "fate worse than death." A schematic morality concluded that if such and such is a fate worse than death, then to prefer it to death would surely be a heinous sin. The logic of war-makers has extended this not only to the preservation of one's own moral integrity but to the fate of others, even of people on the other side of the earth, whom we do not always bother to consult personally on the subject. We weigh the arguments that they are not able to understand (perhaps they have not even heard that arguments exist!). And we decide, in their place, that it is better for them to be dead—killed by us—than Red, living under our enemies.

The Asian whose future we are about to decide is either a bad guy or a good guy. If he is a bad guy, he obviously has to be killed. If he is a good guy, he is on our side and he ought to be ready to die for freedom. We will provide an opportunity for him to do so: we will kill him to prevent him falling under the tyranny of a demonic enemy. Thus we not only defend his interests together with our own, but we protect his virtue along with our own. Think what might happen if he fell under Communist rule *and liked it!*

The advantages of this kind of logic are no exclusive possession of the United States. This is purely and simply the logic shared by all war-makers. It is the logic of *power*. Possibly American generals are naïve enough to push this logic, without realizing, to absurd conclusions. But all who love power tend to think in some such way. Remember Hitler weeping over the ruins of Warsaw after it had been demolished by the Luftwaffe: "How wicked these people must have been," he sobbed, "to make me do this to them!"

Words like "pacification" and "liberation" have acquired sinister connotations as war has succeeded war. Vietnam has done much to refine and perfect these notions. A "free zone" is now one in which anything that moves is assumed to be "enemy" and can be shot. In order to create a "free zone" that can live up effectively to its name, one must level everything, buildings, vegetation, everything, so that one can clearly see anything that moves, and shoot it. This has very interesting semantic consequences.

An American Captain accounts for the levelling of a new "Free Zone" in the following terms: "We want to prevent them from moving freely in this area. . . . From now on anything that moves around here is going to be automatically considered

V.C. and bombed or fired on. The whole Triangle is going to become a Free Zone. These villagers here are all considered hostile civilians."

How did the Captain solve the semantic problem of distinguishing the hostile civilian from the refugee? "In a V.C. area like this there are three categories. First there are the straight V.C. . . . Then there are the V.C. sympathizers. Then there's the . . . There's a third category. . . . I can't think of the third just now but . . . there's no middle road in this war." [4]

"Pacification" or "winning the hearts" of the undecided is thus very much simplified. "Soon" says .a news report,[5] "the Government will have no need to win the hearts and minds of Bensuc. There will be no Bensuc." But there are further simplifications. A "high-ranking U.S. Field commander is quoted as saying: 'If the people are to the guerrillas as oceans are to the fish . . . we are going to dry up that ocean.' " [6] Merely by existing, a civilian, in this context, becomes a "hostile civilian." But at the same time and by the same token he is our friend and our ally. What simpler way out of the dilemma than to destroy him to "save American lives"?

V

So much for the practical language of the battlefield. Let us now attend to the much more pompous and sinister jargon of the war mandarins in government offices and military think-tanks. Here we have a whole community of intellectuals, scholars who spend their time playing out "scenarios" and considering "acceptable levels" in megadeaths. Their language and their thought are as esoteric, as self-enclosed, as tautologous as the advertisement we have just discussed. But instead of being "coifed" in a sweet smell, they are scientifically antiseptic, businesslike, uncontaminated with sentimental concern for life—other than their own. It is the same basic narcissism, but in a masculine, that is, managerial, mode. One proves one's realism along with one's virility by toughness in playing statistically with global death. It is this playing with death, however, that brings into the players' language itself the corruption of death: not physical but mental and moral extinction. And the corruption spreads from their talk, their thinking, to the words and minds of everybody. What happens then is that the political and moral values they claim to be defending are destroyed by the *contempt* that is more and more evident in the language in which they talk about such things. Technological strategy becomes an end in

4. See Jonathan Schell in *The New Yorker* (July 15, 1967), p. 59.
5. *The New York Times,* January 11, 1967.
6. Quoted in the *New Statesman* (March 11, 1966).

itself and leads the fascinated players into a maze where finally the very purpose strategy was supposed to serve is itself destroyed. The ambiguity of official war talk has one purpose above all: to mask this ultimate unreason and permit the game to go on.

Of special importance is the *style* of these nuclear mandarins. The technological puckishness of Herman Kahn is perhaps the classic of this genre. He excels in the sly understatement of the inhuman, the apocalyptic, enormity. His style is esoteric, allusive, yet confidential. The reader has the sense of being a privileged eavesdropper in the councils of the mighty. He knows enough to realize that things are going to happen about which he can do nothing, though perhaps he can save his skin in a properly equipped shelter where he may consider at leisure the rationality of survival in an unlivable world. Meanwhile, the cool tone of the author and the reassuring solemnity of his jargon seem to suggest that those in power, those who turn loose these instruments of destruction, have no intention of perishing themselves, that consequently survival must have a point. The point is not revealed, except that nuclear war is somehow implied to be good business. Nor are H-bombs necessarily a sign of cruel intentions. They enable one to enter into communication with the high priests in the enemy camp. They permit the decision-makers on both sides to engage in a ritual "test of nerve." In any case, the language of escalation is the language of naked power, a language that is all the more persuasive because it is proud of being ethically illiterate and because it accepts, as realistic, the basic irrationality of its own tactics. The language of escalation, in its superb mixture of banality and apocalypse, science and unreason, is the expression of a massive death wish. We can only hope that this death wish is only that of a decaying Western civilization, and that it is not common to the entire race. Yet the language itself is given universal currency by the mass media. It can quickly contaminate the thinking of everybody.

VI

Sartre speaks of the peculiar, expert negligence of the language used by European mandarins (bankers, politicians, prelates), the "indolent and consummate art" they have of communicating with one another in double-talk that leaves them always able to escape while their subordinates are firmly caught.[7] On others, ambiguous directives are imposed with full authority. For others, these are final and inescapable. The purpose of the language game is then to maintain a certain balance of ambiguity and of authority so that the subject is caught and the official is not. Thus the subject can always be proved wrong and the official is always right. The offical is enabled to lie in such a way that

7. *Op. cit.*, p. 202.

if the lie is discovered, a subordinate takes the blame. So much for European democracy. The same has been true in America in a somewhat different context—that of wheeler-dealing and political corruption rather than the framework of authoritarian and official privilege. But power in America, we find, can become mean, belligerent, temperamental. American power, while paying due respect to the demands of plain egalitarian folksiness, has its moments of arbitrary bad humor. But lest this bad humor become too evident, and lest repression begin to seem too forceful, language is at hand as an instrument of manipulation. Once again, the use of language to extol freedom, democracy, and equal rights, while at the same time denying them, causes words to turn sour and to rot in the minds of those who use them. In such a context, the effort of someone such as Lenny Bruce to restore to language some of its authentic impact was a service despairingly offered to a public that could not fully appreciate it. One might argue that the language of this disconcerting and perhaps prophetic comedian was often less obscene than the "decent" but horrifying platitudes of those who persecuted him.

VII

Michel Foucault has described the evolution of the dialogue between medicine and madness in the Age of Reason.[8] Therapeutic experiments with manic-depressives in the eighteenth century assumed a certain inner consistency in the delirium of the mad and, working within the suppressed framework of this consistency, sought to suggest to the madman an alternative to his madness—or, rather, to push the "logic" of his madness to a paroxysm and crisis in which it would be confronted with itself and "forced to argue against the demands of its own truth." Thus, for instance, in cases of religious mania and despair, patients who believed themselves damned were shown a theatrical tableau in which the avenging angel appeared, punished, and then gave assurance that guilt was now taken away. Patients who were dying of starvation because, believing themselves dead, they would not eat were shown representations of dead persons eating and were thus brought face to face with an unexpected syllogism: you claim you are dead and cannot eat, but dead men can eat. . . . The beauty of Foucault's book is that we become fascinated by the way in which the "reason" of the Age of Englightenment unconsciously shared so much of the madness with which it was in dialogue.

Reading of this dialogue between reason and madness, one is reminded of the language of power and war. In the deliberate, realistic madness of the new language we find an implicit admission that words, ordinary discourse, won't do—not exactly that language itself has

8. Michel Foucault, *Madness and Civilization* (New York: 1967), p. 188.

broken down, is no longer valid as such. But the enemy is at once so perverse and so irrational—such a psychopathic liar in fact—that he has to be cleverly treated as a beast or as a maniac. We all know that it is customary for one who resorts to violence to do so on the ground that the adversary "does not understand anything else." The "language of escalation" is a more sophisticated application of this principle, but on a massive scale implemented by the threat of a nuclear strike. It seems, indeed, that since the adversary understands nothing but force, and since force means everything up to and including the use of H-bombs, we will eventually get beyond the mere threat of a nuclear strike: one of us will actually strike. This will demonstrate that if you face an enemy with the conviction that he understands nothing but force, you will yourself necessarily behave as if you understood nothing but force. And in fact it is highly probable that if you say he understands nothing but force, it is because you yourself are already in the same plight.

In any case, it is quite obvious that the military on whatever side must be quite convinced of the superior efficacy of force, or they would not be military. If they worry about this at all, they can always reason that force is necessary because we are faced by various bunches of madmen who understand nothing else. The dialogue then proceeds in a way that reminds us of Foucault:

1. Rational discourse with the enemy is useless. He does not understand rational discourse and makes negotiation an opportunity for lying and pathological trickery. He *has to* cheat.

2. Therefore he has to be dealt with solely in the framework of his madness and wickedness, his propensity to lie and cheat. One does not bargain with such a one, because bargaining implies the acceptance, on both sides, of conditions. He must be pushed to the point where his surrender is unconditional in terms of his own madness. To grant him reasonable conditions would be to treat a madman as a rational being, which would be the worst possible kind of mistake and indeed (if you believe in sin) a sin.

3. His madness has roots in guilt, because he is, after all, wicked. He understands *punishment*. But the punishment must be shown to him in terms of his own madness. He must see that his own destructive violence will lead inexorably to one consequence: his own annihilation. But to translate this into words would lead to confusion. The message must be got to him in the unmistakable language of force itself. Of course, verbal formulas have to be resorted to, in order to define what force is all about, to set conditions, etc. But the verbal formulas must be kept deliberately ambiguous, unclear. The clear and unmistakable message is not that of the *terms offered* but of the escalation itself. In other words there is an *appearance* of dialogue on the verbal and political level. But the real dialogue is with weapons and may be a complete contradiction of what appears to be said in the prose of politics.

The effect of this, of course, is a vicious circle: it begins with a tacit admission that negotiation is meaningless, and it does in fact render the language of negotiation meaningless. War-makers in the twentieth century have gone far toward creating a political language so obscure, so apt for treachery, so ambiguous, that it can no longer serve as an instrument for peace: it is good only for war. But why? Because the language of the war-maker is *self-enclosed in finality*. It does not invite reasonable dialogue, it uses language to silence dialogue, to block communication, so that instead of words the two sides may trade divisions, positions, villages, air bases, cities—and of course the lives of the people in them. The daily toll of the killed (or the "kill ratio") is perfunctorily scrutinized and decoded. And the totals are expertly managed by "ministers of truth" so that the newspaper reader may get the right message.

Our side is always ahead. He who is winning must be the one who is right. But we are right, therefore we must be winning. Once again we have the beautiful, narcissistic tautology of war—or of advertising. Once again, "Arpège has Arpège." There is no communicating with anyone else, because anyone who does not agree, who is outside the charmed circle, is wrong, is evil, is already in hell.

VIII

It is a dictum of Marxism that a word is true if it can be verified by being carried out in action. But this idea is not a monopoly of the Communists. It is now universal. It is everybody's property. Modern politics is a matter of defining how you think things ought to be and then making them come out that way by cunning or by force. If you aren't strong enough or smart enough to verify your ideas by putting them into effect, then you have no business saying how things should be in the first place: follow somebody else who has the necessary power! The strange thing is that this idea is not so modern after all. In fact it is quite ancient. Another word for it is magic, or witchcraft.

Of course, the shaman and the medicine man in primitive society did not possess the advantages of a technological skill that would enable them to say that white was black and then prove the point by turning white into black. Yet even unlimited power does not always succeed in making one's own words come true—as the Vietnam war has conclusively shown.

One of the most curious things about the war in Vietnam is that it is being *fought to vindicate the assumptions upon which it is being fought*. Now it turns out that these American assumptions are quite wrong: the White House and the Pentagon have consistently interpreted the war as a military invasion of South Vietnam by the North. In other words it is the Korean War over again, a "conventional limited war" in which the problems are above all military and can be handled in terms of bombing, sending in more troops, wiping out areas in which the enemy tends to concentrate, cutting supply lines, etc. By the escalation of the war and the bombing of North Vietnam (after the "Tonkin Bay Incident," which has now been shown to have been exaggerated if not actually faked) the United States did actually turn the war into the kind of war it was supposed to be in America—apart from the fact that the aggression was the other way around. But this did nothing to alter the fact that the war in the South remained essentially a revolutionary guerrilla struggle that could not be adequately handled by conventional military operations.

Alastair Buchan, analyzing this curious fact in *Encounter*,[9] wonders how it was possible for such a policy to be accepted when the U.S. government relies on "a wide range of research institutes and universities to give greater depth and accuracy to its own operational and political analysis." He hazards a guess that the unassailable self-confidence of science somehow contributed to the error: "Probably technology (helicopters, new small arms, infra-red sensors and all the rest) was the element that corrupted judgement, making it seem possible that the Americans could do what the natives (i.e. the South Vietnamese army) or the old colonial powers (e.g. the French) could not." In other words, there is a certain hubris built into technological thinking that encloses it within itself and its own suppositions and makes it fatally ignore decisive realities that do not fit those suppositions.

However, in such a situation, power can still vindicate itself by *declaring* that its estimate was the correct one and that it is still winning. Since statistics can be made to prove anything, it adduces statistics to show that its words are in fact coming true. Unfortunately, the Tet offensive of the Vietcong in 1968 made it finally clear that no amount of juggling with words or figures could make this "politics of inadvertence" (the words of Arthur Schlesinger's) come out level with reality. Lyndon Johnson is certainly well versed in all the appropriate skills, and yet in this instance he turned out to be a singularly failed witch.

What needs to be noted is that the massive effort of the United States to gain acceptance for its own version of the Vietnam war by doing all in its power to turn that version into accomplished fact has had profoundly significant effects. And these effects are not what was intended. Confidence in the Washington government, in the American political system, in the credibility of American officials, even in the basic human integrity and sincerity of the American Establishment is now seriously undermined at home and abroad. The *political language* of the United States, which was suspect before, has now been fatally denatured. It has probably lost all its value as intellectual currency. The crisis of the dollar is intimately connected with the crisis of human communication that has resulted from the sinister double-talk of the American Establishment about itself, about the war, about the

9. January–February, 1968.

race situation, about the urgent domestic problems that are being ignored or set aside while the government puts more and more money and manpower into the war. The tragedy is not so much that America has come out of its pristine isolationism but that it has decided to rule the world without paying serious attention to anybody else's view of what the world is all about. Language has been distorted and denatured in defense of this solipsistic, this basically isolationist and sometimes even paranoid, attitude.

IX

What next? The illness of political language—which is almost universal and is a symptom of a Plague of Power that is common to China and America, Russia and Western Europe—is characterized everywhere by the same sort of double-talk, tautology, ambiguous cliché, self-righteous and doctrinaire pomposity, and pseudoscientific jargon that mask a total callousness and moral insensitivity, indeed a basic contempt for man. The self-enclosed finality that bars all open dialogue and pretends to impose absolute conditions of one's own choosing upon everybody else ultimately becomes the language of totalist dictatorship, if it is not so already. Revolt against this is taking the form of another, more elemental and anarchistic, kind of violence, together with a different semantic code. Space does not permit us to study this other language, but it must be acknowledged as immensely popular and influential all over the world. It is the language of Che Guevara, of Régis Debray, of Frantz Fanon: the violent language and the apocalyptic myth of the guerrilla warrior, the isolated individual and the small group, enabled by revolutionary charisma to defy all the technological might of the biggest powers in the world. In spite of the failure of Che in Bolivia—a failure that only resulted in his canonization as a martyr of the post-colonial revolution—the Vietnam war has had the result of awakening revolutionary hopes all over the world, from Harlem to Angola. Che Guevara called for Vietnams everywhere, and the Black Power movement, introducing the language of Fanon into American political life, is set on making the inner cities of the United States "other Vietnams." At the moment, when the full tragedy has not yet manifested itself, this might to some seem an inspiring revolt against the inhuman pride of technological white power. But the hopes of Fanon—which may have some basis in the jungles of Africa—are couched in the same terms of magic and witchcraft that assert something and then proceed to make it so in fact, thereby vindicating their own prophecy. If this went wrong for U.S. power in Vietnam, it may also go wrong in the American ghettos, where, unfortunately, the Negro does not have miles of swamp and jungle to maneuver in but is enclosed in a small and highly vulnerable area in which he can easily be destroyed or arrested and taken off to concentration camps.

However that may be, the revolutionary tactic that tends to harass and immobolize the Goliath of technological military power and bring it down largely by its own elephantine weight has at the same time created a new language that mocks the ponderous and self-important utterances of the Establishment. This new language, racy, insolent, direct, profane, iconoclastic, and earthy, may have its own magic incantation and myth. It may be involved in its own elaborate set of illusions. But at least it represents a healthier and more concrete style of thought. It does not reduce everything to abstractions, and though it is fully as intransigent as the language of the Establishment, it still seems to be more in contact with relevant experience: the hard realities of poverty, brutality, vice, and resistance.

Yet, flexible though it might be in some respects, it remains another language of power, therefore of self-enclosed finality, which rejects dialogue and negotiation on the axiomatic supposition that the adversary is a devil with whom no dialogue is possible.

Nhat Hanh Is My Brother

This is not a political statement. It has no "interested" motive, it seeks to provoke no immediate reaction "for" or "against" this or that side in the Vietnam war. It is on the contrary a human and personal statement and an anguished plea for the Vietnamese Buddhist monk Thich Nhat Hanh who is my brother. He is more my brother than many who are nearer to me by race and nationality, because he and I see things exactly the same way. He and I deplore the war that is ravaging his country. We deplore it for exactly the same reasons: human reasons, reasons of sanity, justice and love. We deplore the needless destruction, the fantastic and callous ravaging of human life, the rape of the culture and spirit of an exhausted people. It is surely evident that this carnage serves no purpose that can be discerned and indeed contradicts the alleged intentions of the mighty nation that has constituted itself the "defender" of the people it is destroying.

Certainly this statement cannot help being a plea for peace. But it is also a plea for my brother Nhat Hanh. He represents the least "political" of all the movements in Vietnam. He is not directly associated with the Buddhists who are trying to use political manipulation in order to save their country. He is by no means a Communist. The Vietcong is deeply hostile to him. He refuses to be identified with the established government which hates and distrusts him. He represents the young, the defenseless, the new ranks of youth who find themselves with every hand turned against them except those of the peasants and the poor, with whom they are working. Nhat Hanh speaks truly for the people of Vietnam, if there can be said to be a "people" still left in Vietnam.

Nhat Hanh has left his country and has come to us in order to present a picture which is not given us in our newspapers and magazines. He has been well received—and that speaks well for those who have received him. His visit to the United States has shown that we are a people who still desire the truth when we can find it, and still decide in favor of *man* against the political machine when we get a fair chance to do so. But when Nhat Hanh goes home, what will happen to him? He is not in favor with the government which has suppressed his writings. The Vietcong will view with disfavor his American contacts. To have pleaded for an end to the fighting will make him a traitor in the eyes of those who stand to gain personally as long as the war goes on, as long as their countrymen are being killed, as long as they can do business with our military. Nhat Hanh may be returning to imprisonment, torture, even death. We cannot let him go back to Saigon to be destroyed while we sit here, cherishing the warm humanitarian glow of good intentions and worthy sentiments about the ongoing war. We who have met and heard Nhat Hanh, or who have read about him, must also raise our voices to demand that his life and freedom be respected when he returns to his country. Furthermore, we demand this not in terms of any conceivable political advantage, but purely in the name of those values of freedom and humanity in favor of which our armed forces declare they are fighting the Vietnam war.

Nhat Hanh is a free man who has acted as a free man in favor of his brothers and moved by the spiritual dynamic of a tradition of religious compassion. He has come among us as many others have, from time to time, bearing witness to the spirit of Zen. More than any other he has shown us that Zen is not an esoteric and world-denying cult of inner illumination, but that it has its rare and unique sense of responsibility in the modern world. Wherever he goes he will walk in the strength of his spirit and in the solitude of the Zen monk who sees beyond life and death. It is for our own honor as much as for his safety that we must raise our voices to demand that his life and personal integrity be fully respected when he returns to his smashed and gutted country, there to continue his work with the students and peasants, hoping for the day when reconstruction can begin.

I have said Nhat Hanh is my brother, and it is true. We are both monks, and we have lived the monastic life about the same number of years. We are both poets, both existentialists. I have far more in common with Nhat Hanh than I have with many Americans, and I do not hesitate to say it. It is vitally important that such bonds be admitted. They are the bonds of a new solidarity and a new brotherhood which is beginning to be evident on all the five continents and which cuts across all political, religious and cultural lines to unite young men and women in every country in something that is more concrete than an ideal and more alive than a program. This unity of the young is the only hope of the world. In its name I appeal for Nhat Hanh. Do what you can for him. If I mean something to you, then let me put it this way: do for Nhat Hanh whatever you would do for me if I were in his position. In many ways I wish I were.

Prayer for Peace

Almighty and merciful God, Father of all men, Creator and Ruler of the Universe, Lord of History, whose designs are inscrutable, whose glory is without blemish, whose compassion for the errors of men is inexhaustible, in your will is our peace!

Mercifully hear this prayer which rises to you from the tumult and desperation of a world in which you are forgotten, in which your name is not invoked, your laws are derided and your presence is ignored. Because we do not know you, we have no peace.

From the heart of an eternal silence, you have watched the rise of empires and have seen the smoke of their downfall.

You have seen Egypt, Assyria, Babylon, Greece and Rome, once powerful, carried away like sand in the wind.

You have witnessed the impious fury of ten thousand fratricidal wars, in which great powers have torn whole continents to shreds in the name of peace and justice.

And now our nation itself stands in imminent danger of a war the like of which has never been seen!
This nation dedicated to freedom, not to power,
Has obtained, through freedom, a power it did not desire.

And seeking by that power to defend its freedom, it is enslaved by the processes and policies of power.
Must we wage a war we do not desire, a war that can do us no good,
And which our very hatred of war forces us to prepare?

A day of ominous decision has now dawned on this free nation.
Armed with a titanic weapon, and convinced of our own right,

We face a powerful adversary, armed with the same weapon, equally convinced that he is right.

In this moment of destiny, this moment we never foresaw, we cannot afford to fail.
Our choice of peace or war may decide our judgment and publish it in an eternal record.

In this fatal moment of choice in which we might begin the patient architecture of peace
We may also take the last step across the rim of chaos.

Save us then from our obsessions! Open our eyes, dissipate our confusions, teach us to understand ourselves and our adversary!
Let us never forget that sins against the law of love are punished by loss of faith,
And those without faith stop at no crime to achieve their ends!

Help us to be masters of the weapons that threaten to master us.
Help us to use our science for peace and plenty, not for war and destruction.
Show us how to use atomic power to bless our children's children, not to blight them.

Save us from the compulsion to follow our adversaries in all that we most hate, confirming them in their hatred and suspicion of us.
Resolve our inner contradictions, which now grow beyond belief and beyond bearing.
They are at once a torment and a blessing: for if you had not left us the light of conscience, we would not have to endure them.

Teach us to be long-suffering in anguish and insecurity.

Teach us to wait and trust.
Grant light, grant strength and patience to all who work for peace,
To this Congress, our President, our military forces, and our adversaries.

Grant us prudence in proportion to our power,
Wisdom in proportion to our science,
Humaneness in proportion to our wealth and might.
And bless our earnest will to help all races and peoples to travel, in friendship with us,
Along the road to justice, liberty and lasting peace:
But grant us above all to see that our ways are not necessarily your ways,
That we cannot fully penetrate the mystery of your designs

And that the very storm of power now raging on this earth
Reveals your hidden will and your inscrutable decision.
Grant us to see your face in the lightning of this cosmic storm,
O God of holiness, mercifuul to men:
Grant us to seek peace where it is truly found!

In your will, O God, is our peace!
Amen

This prayer, written by T. Merton, was read in the House of Representatives by Congressman Frank Kowalski (D. Connecticut) on April 12, 1962 (Wednesday in Holy Week).